Geropsychology:
A Model of Training
and Clinical Service

Geropsychology:
A Model of Training
and Clinical Service

W. Doyle Gentry, Ph.D.
Duke University Medical Center
Durham, North Carolina

Ballinger Publishing Company • Cambridge, Massachusetts
A Subsidiary of J.B. Lippincott Company

International Standard Book Number: 0-88410-503-2

Library of Congress Catalog Card Number: 76-48949

Printed in the United States of America

Library of Congress Cataloging in Publication Data
Main entry under title:

Geropsychology.

Bibliography: p.
1. Aged—Psychology—Addresses, essays, lectures. 2. Clinical psychology—Addresses, essays, lectures. I. Gentry, William Doyle, 1943- [DNLM: 1. Aging. 2. Models, Psychological. 3. Psychology, Clinical—In old age. WT150 G377]
BF724.8.G46   155.67   76-48949
ISBN 0-88410-503-2

Dedication

To
Lillian and John Hamilton, with love

Contents

Preface

On June 13 and 14, 1974, a conference co-sponsored by the Duke University Center for the Study of Aging and Human Development and the Division of Medical Psychology, Department of Psychiatry, at the Duke University Medical Center was held on the topic of "Geropsychology: A Model of Training and Clinical Service". The conference was unusual in that it may well have represented the first organized attempt to investigate the actual or potential role of the profession of clinical psychology in providing mental health services to older persons in this country. Prior to this, and even today, there was an obvious neglect by clinical psychologists in diagnosing and treating the aged. The professional literature dealing with psychological services to the aged is meager, fragmented, and speaks more to the issue of "what might or should be done" than what is actually being done for the elderly. Graduate training and internship training programs simply do not, for the most part, provide any clinical experiences for psychologists with older persons except in institutionalized settings, do not focus on age as a separate or important variable in understanding normal and abnormal behavior, and do not generally take a life-span developmental approach toward viewing changes in human behavior over time. As one leading psychologist in the field of aging put it, "Clinical psychology seems to have missed the boat with respect to services to the aged." and in fact lags far behind the professions of psychiatry, nursing, sociology, and social work in this regard.

The two-day conference attempted to examine such issues as the need for new and different models in professional psychology, the role(s) of clinical psychology in mental health programming for the aged in state institutions, and the need for additional psychological services for the aged as viewed by persons in the legislature. It focused specifically on a professional role model for clinical psychologists working with the elderly, the *geropsychologist*. The role of the geropsychologist, it was suggested, should incorporate traditional clinical skills such as psychological testing and psychotherapy with the more innovative functions of community care manager and government policy maker. The geropsychologist should be flexible in providing several services simultaneously, should be able to cooperate with other mental health professionals in serving the elderly, and should most importantly spend most of his or her energies out in the community where 95 percent of persons over sixty-five years of age reside, rather than in isolated institutional settings.

The conference also examined the impact of psychological treatment programs for the aged, based on evaluation of past efforts, and focused on a "behavioral model" approach toward treating abnormal behavior in older persons as one alternative to the more universally held "medical or illness model" applied to the aged. It looked at what may be a more appropriate psychological theory of the later years, C.G. Jung's so-called theory of the *second half of life*, at the relevance of the life-span developmental psychology literature for clinical training and service to the aged, and at an active, innovative model of community geropsychology. Finally, a curriculum for training geropsychologists, or more broadly conceived professionals interested in clinical gerontology, which incorporated most of the above was presented.

This book represents the proceedings of this conference. It is being published in an effort to reach a larger audience than was present at the conference in 1972 and to serve as a catalyst for greater interest and activity by clinical psychologists in the field of aging. This book is not meant to be *the* answer to the vacuum of psychological services to the aged in this country; it will not "create magically the large numbers of geropsychologists who are needed" to fill the needs of the elderly in today's society. Rather, we hope it will serve as a legitimate first effort in this area and will give clinical psychologists who read it something to constructively and positively react to, perhaps in the way of suggesting additional service roles which we were unaware of or new elements of a geropsychology curriculum which we overlooked.

I am indebted to my colleagues who participated in the conference and who subsequently authored individual chapters for this book. Their patience along with their continued interest and encouragement were most appreciated. I am particularly grateful to Dr. Ilene Seigler for her help in pulling the various chapters together and for her enthusiastic commitment to seeing this project through to its completion. I am also indebted to Dr. George Maddox, Director of the Duke University Center for the Study of Aging and Human Development, for his support both in funding the conference and in continually stressing the potentially vital role for clinical psychologists in the field of aging. Last but not least, I am thankful to the fifty five persons—psychologists, psychiatrists, nurses, and other mental health professionals—who attended the conference and whose encouraging comments afterwards served as the impetus for this text.

The conference was funded through a grant from the Administration on Aging, No. 94P 203 84/4, Department of Health, Education and Welfare.

W. Doyle Gentry

Foreword

The limits of human rationality are substantial. This is hardly news to clinicians in the helping professions; their clients and patients frequently exhibit incongruities between what they know, what they feel, and what they do. The chapters in this book make a point that, while it may not be news to clinical psychologists, is nonetheless a point worth making: There are incongruities in what clinical psychologists know about, feel about, and do about older people who need psychological care. The incongruities are a matter of record.

A great deal has been learned about aging and the aged during the past quarter of a century. The numbers of older persons are large and are growing at a rapid rate. In the United States, over 20 million persons are 65 years of age and older; twice this many are 55 years of age and older; about seven million persons are 75 years of age or older. The probability of physical and psychological impairment is a function of age, and it follows that older persons have elevated needs for health and welfare services. As a rule of thumb, older persons consume health and welfare services at a rate three times as high as adults generally. As one illustration of special needs for care in late life, long term chronic care beds, usually occupied by older persons, now outnumber acute care beds in the United States. The risk of institutionalization is a function of age, although we now know that institutionalization frequently reflects social and professional conveniences as much as demonstrated personal need.

While the demonstrated need for care in late life is great, we do know that prevailing negative stereotypes of aging and the aged have been exaggerated and are substantially inaccurate. In the absence of debilitating disease, intellectual functioning characterizes most older persons well into their seventies and, for many, much beyond that. Organic brain syndromes, although a function of age in late life, nonetheless are the exception rather than the rule. The causal undifferentiated diagnosis of many older persons as senile, demented, or organic on the basis of inadequate evidence is scandalously common. The lack of proper psychological care both in community and institutional settings is a national disgrace. Neither theory nor evidence can justify the observed neglect.

Are psychologists unaware of the needs of older persons for providing such care? This is possible, but difficult to comprehend. There has been a section on adult development and aging in the American Psychological Association for 30 years. There have been three White House Conferences on Aging, the most recent in 1971, which outlined the needs and opportunities for psychological care of older persons in elaborate detail. Recent federal legislation on community mental health centers notes the historic neglect of older people and mandates corrective action. The National Institute of Mental Health belatedly has created a Center for the Study of the Mental Health of the Aged.

The belatedness of these developments surely reflect the peculiar American preoccupation with youthfulness. But they also illustrate the myopia of psychological theories of development that somehow managed to fixate on childhood and adolescence. And professional leadership is also implicated. Reality has been suspended long enough. It is time for someone to demand, not suggest, that training in clinical psychology include care of older persons in the curriculum.

This volume lays the foundation for such a demand by reviewing the theory, research, and clinical experience that makes the psychological care of older persons seem sensible and feasible. The imperative to act has been present for a long time. Welcome to the authors of this volume, who have good ideas about how to respond and are translating these ideas effectively into action. Psychological care of older persons in the last quarter of the twentieth century should be better than it has been. It can be better. This volume provides a basis for expecting that the psychological care of older persons in the future will be better.

George L. Maddox

Chapter 1

Clinical Psychology and Aging: A Role Model

Leonard E. Gottesman
Philadelphia Geriatric Center

Clinical psychology has until now offered a "mixed message" to professionals interested in working clinically with the aging and aged. It has, in fact, offered very little in the way of a role model for psychological activities with this population. On the one hand, the mainstream of clinical psychology has had very little concern for older individuals. If one looks at the development of psychology historically, one is quick to note the early movement of psychology toward the problems of psychological testing and diagnosis. However, one is also quick to note that this movement was stimulated by a basic concern by Binet and others that school age children be properly placed in the school environment with respect to their intellectual abilities. The same concern, the concern of "doing the right thing for the child," and the whole business of education served as a second historical movement for clinical psychology, highlighted by the writings of Hull, Skinner, and many others. These psychologists were themselves teachers, and their primary concern was how to provide better education for children and young people.

Furthermore, most psychologists, when they teach about human development, use themselves and their children as examples. They focus on their own life experience, their own view of the world, as a basis for educating others. This has also led to less of a concern for problems of the aged because: (1) psychologists—like all adult human beings—are unclear about their own feelings and relationships with older people (e.g., their parents), and (2) they are equally unclear about their own feelings about aging themselves. In short, their own difficulty in dealing with the process of aging has prevented problems of the aged from becoming part of the educational concerns of the profession.

Even the concern by clinical psychology about mental illness, which has shaped so much of psychological practice, has in reality centered around a concern about mental illness in young or at best middle-aged adults. Historically, the greatest growth in clinical psychological services came after World War II as part of the Veterans Administration's attempt to provide treatment for returning veterans, who for the most part were young men. Even counseling and psychotherapy activities have grown primarily in response to needs of our students, our colleagues, our friends, and even ourselves, rather than in response to older persons, with whom we were less familiar. This restrictiveness of clinical interest was supported by Freud's notion that analysis was wasted on rigid, mature people who had short lives before them and also, interestingly enough, by older people themselves, who prefer consulting a minister or physician when they have a problem of psychological nature, rather than a psychiatrist or psychologist.

What has been the result of this lack of concern by clinical psychology for problems of aging and the aged? Well for one thing, there are currently over 20 million people in the United States over 65 years of age (10 percent of the total population) and by the turn of the century there may well be over 40 million people in this population. For the most part, these people are underserved with respect to psychological services (Lawton and Gottesman, 1974). Many of these people need psychological services, in part because of our failures in treatment programs in mental hospitals and nursing homes (Gottesman, 1971). The latter is extremely important since every one of the one million nursing home patients in this country are geriatric and 50–80 percent of them have a diagnosable mental disorder. In effect, what we have is a population who are at a new stage of life, who simply weren't around at the time clinical psychology came into being as a profession but who now very probably are suffering from this lack of concern. Another result of this lack of interest is that we do not have any personality theories that deal adequately with aging and the aged; we do not know much about the capacity for learning in older people; and, we have very few clinicians who are suitably trained and are comfortable in dealing with the aged. In short, as a profession, we are ill equipped to meet the challenge at hand.

I should emphasize that psychology as a whole has not completely neglected the field of aging. On the contrary, there has been a continuing thread of interest by psychologists over the years in this population, although primarily not among persons of the clinical persuasion. For example, in 1922, G. Stanley Hall published his book on *Senescence*, and even before that Galton was measuring behavioral characteristics of people across the entire age span including the elderly. Many other psychologists in recent years have figured prominently in the emerging field of gerontology, including people such as Kleemier, Thomas, Birren, Kullem, Wilma Donahue, Joseph Butten, Walter Obrist, and Carl Eisdorfer, as well as the other contributors to this volume. Several leading universities and medical schools have also been traditionally represented by virtue of the high and continued interest of their psychology faculty in problems of the aged. These include, among others, University of Chicago, University of Michigan, Columbia University, Wisconsin University, Duke University Medical Center, and the University of Southern California.

I also do not wish to suggest that psychology as a whole has not made many vital contributions to the field of aging and the problems of the aged. Nothing could be further from the truth. I think it is safe to say that while gerontology may not have been a central concern for psychologists, psychology and the contributions of psychologists have been of central concern to gerontology. At least three major contributions by psychology to the field of aging should be noted. First, the basic research of psychologists interested in aging has stressed the importance of the interaction between human physiology and behavioral changes resulting from aging. That is, psychologists have clearly demonstrated that what happens in the central nervous system and elsewhere throughout the body really is important in determining how the older individual interacts with his environment, his ability to learn, and so forth. Second, the work of psychologists has emphasized the relationship between the aged and their social milieu and has noted the importance of collaborative efforts by psychologists, economists, sociologists, and professionals from a variety of other disciplines necessary to gain a more complete picture of the aging process and its effect on the human being. Third, and perhaps most important, psychologists have introduced measurement and a concern for objective evaluation not previously there into the field of aging and aging research. They have, for example, provided a methodology for studying life span development and have emphasized the important differences in results obtained from cross-sectional versus longitudinal studies of aging.

Where psychology has not contributed and thus had an impact has been, as I noted previously, in the area of clinical service (Lawton and Gottesman, 1974). Let me now suggest a few roles the psychologist might play in this area. First, and probably most obvious, is the role of psychological tester—test maker and test giver. The Social Security Administration, for example, would like to know who among the millions of aged in this country are mentally competent and who are in need of a representative payee, a protector and guardian to take care of them; they would like a test devised that would screen the aged on social security and make this determination. Similarly, the federal government and several state governments would like to know who among the aged require nursing home care and whether such care is needed on a skilled or intermediated (and thus less expensive) level; again, they would like a test devised to make this decision. These are important questions, and the challenge for psychologists to respond to this type of need is great. There are, however, also great dangers involved in this type of test construction and administration, which Powell Lawton and I have discussed elsewhere (Lawton and Gottesman, 1974), and which one should consider before embarking along these lines of service. Other contributions the psychological tester could make are potentially less problematic—that is, providing answers to specific questions about functional impairment and psychopathology in the aged such as: What type of treatment program(s) are appropriate for a given patient? Does the patient require institutional care and, if he does, what type? Are there alternatives to institutional care for this individual; what are they? How long will the aged patient require treatment and how will we know when he has received maximum benefit from treatment? These seem to be fair questions, but questions that are not likely to be answered via traditional psychological tests as they have or have not been applied to the aged (Lawton, 1970). New tests will obviously have to be constructed and new considerations also given to the problems of administering tests to older persons who may in reality be both distrustful of psychological tests and also characterized by a tendency toward response inhibition in performing such tests (Gentry, 1970).

A second role is that of therapist or listener. The deeply felt problems and concerns of every maturing person are appropriate areas for both individual and group psychotherapy. The aged have obvious need for help in dealing with problems associated with retirement, widowhood, death, psychosomatic illness, and learning new skills for a second career. These are problems that are often very frightening, for which the older person may not be at all prepared, and which require drastic change on his part. One need only survey the psychiatric literature on aging (Busse and Pfeiffer, 1969) to understand the enormous opportunity for therapeutic service in this population. Contrary to Freud's notion about rigidity in the aged, old age is a time of dynamic, active, and often imposed change and instability; perhaps during this period of life more than ever before, the individual needs someone professional to listen, counsel, and advise.

A third and related role involves the development of behavior modification and milieu treatment programs for treating the aged, primarily in institutions. These particular treatment modalities historically were developed by psychologists and rely on psychological principles for their execution. These programs were initially devised for treating mentally ill patients, but it was quickly noted that most of the mentally ill in institutions were in fact also elderly. Thus, quite accidentally, psychology acquired a history of successfully treating the aged along these lines. Related to this is the role of the psychologist as ward manager. Psychologists in the VA system have been serving as ward administrators or ward chiefs since shortly after World War II and have done quite well at this task. This role, that of a leader of a multidisciplinary treatment team, is one that could easily be expanded into nursing homes throughout this country today. It is imperative, however, that any psychologist who accepts this role learn to understand and treat the physical as well as social and psychological aspects of the residents' problems if he is to be truly effective in this regard.

A fourth role for the clinical psychologist serving the aged is that of care manager in the community (Lawton and Gottesman, 1974). In this role, the psychologist must become aware of and must interact with resource agencies and persons in a community setting in an effort to service multiple needs of a population of aged persons. This includes liaison with private practitioners, community mental health centers, medical services, nutrition programs, senior citizen housing programs, institutional programs, and legal advisory services. The psychologist must learn the organizational barriers to effective cooperation among these resources and ways of overcoming these barriers. He must also continue to focus on the needs of the individual client, while at the same time trying to negotiate these complex resources in order to be helpful. A model for this role currently exists at the Philadelphia Geriatric Center, where we are trying to evaluate the needs and wishes for services of 7,000 older persons in a two square mile neighborhood area. In this effort, we are not only interested in encouraging cooperation among existing resource agencies and in developing new services for our clients, but also are considering the cost-benefit ratio for those services we can provide for the aged. Here I serve both as a psychologist interested in and sensitive to the individual needs of my clients, as well as to the need for objective evaluation and measurement in every aspect of the program, and also as the overall program manager. The latter role requires that I work with a nurse, a social worker, a research director, and several kinds of paraprofessionals in a coordinated attempt to aid the older individual in coping within the community environment. Thus far, this role has been both challenging and rewarding.

A fifth and final (for the moment) role for clinical psychologists in serving the aged is that of government policymaker. This role comes from the psychologists' investment in research data and program evaluation. Several of my colleagues and I have recently begun to work as consultants to governmental agencies interested in problems of the aged. One of my co-workers noted in his field reports that a great deal of the policy set with governmental bureaucracy is decided on an emotional basis—on feelings rather than on facts. We know, for example, that concern about the size of the public welfare budget is not so much a concern about dollars per se as it is a concern about dollars in relation to perceived values, biases, and program priorities. The welfare budget need only be put up against the defense budget to make this point very clear. Our role as professionals—and this is not only a role for psychologists—is to bring the results of research, concern for individual differences, and an investment in continuous evaluation before bureaucrats. This role is simultaneously one of interpreter of research findings, advocate for a particular point of view, and active change agent. In this role, we have suggested and fought for state regulations governing such services to the aged as day care centers, transportation, protective services, and home health services. In the future, we plan to encourage the organization and cooperation of resource services for elderly persons in a greatly expanded area outside our current two square mile neighborhood described earlier, and thus will hopefully increase the need for psychologists as community care managers.

Having outlined several possible roles for clinical psychologists working with the aged, let me now express two points of concern. First, there is no way to create magically the large numbers of geropsychologists who are needed if we are to adequately fill the psychological needs of the aged in today's society, not to mention tomorrow's. Last year there were 36,000 first admissions of geriatric patients to state hospitals in the United States and an additional 138,000 geriatric patients already in residence in these institutions alone. If each of these 174,000 persons were to have the services of a psychologist for one day per year, at least 700 geropsychologists would be needed. The Division of Adult Development and Aging (Division 20) of the American Psychological Association currently has only 300 members, persons with a definite interest in the psychology of aging, and current funding policies in the federal government seem aimed at restricting educational programs at the graduate level that might produce future psychologists with this particular interest and clinical expertise. Where, then, are we going to get the professional manpower to fill these roles?

Second, clinical psychologists who intend to work with the aged must be paid for their services. However, recent legislation has made psychological services reimbursable only if provided under a physician's order (Lawton and Gottesman, 1974), a condition that is more than likely going to drive those few clinicians interested in working with this population elsewhere.

Both of these concerns will, of course, have a definite bearing on the impact—or lack of it—that clinical psychology makes in aging in future years. Hopefully continuing education requirements for psychologists in practice and changes in the training programs for psychologists in the universities (Lawton and Gottesman, 1974) will correct some of the manpower shortage, while changes in federal and state laws regulating the practice and payment of clinical psychologists will resolve and perhaps reverse the latter concern. One can only be optimistic, and that I am.

REFERENCES

Busse, E.W. and Pfeiffer, E., eds. *Behavior and adaptation in late life.* Boston: Little, Brown, 1969.

Gentry, W.D. The role of the psychologist. In *Guidelines for an information and counseling service for older persons*, pp. 48–51. Durham, N.C.: Duke University Center for the Study of Aging and Human Development, 1970.

Gottesman, L.E. The institutionalized elderly: a new challenge. In G.L. Maddox, ed., *The future of aging and the aged*, pp. 54–68. Atlanta: SNPA Foundation Seminar Books, 1971.

Lawton, M.P. Gerontology in clinical psychology, and vice-versa. *Aging and Human Development*, 1970, *1*: 147–59.

Lawton, M.P. and Gottesman, L.E. Psychological services to the elderly. *American Psychologist*, 1974, *29*: 689–93.

Chapter 2

Perspectives in the Evaluation of Psychological Mental Health Problems for the Aged

Robert L. Kahn
University of Chicago

It is very discouraging to contemplate the history of the mental health care of the aged in this country. No matter what the prevailing system of services, the aged seem to have been systematically relegated to the poorest, most hopeless type of care (Kahn, 1975).

In the first half of this century the mentally ill aged were disproportionately dumped in the custodial care institutions of that time—the state hospital. In New York State, for example, while the rate of first admissions to mental hospitals for all age groups increased from 71 per 100,000 population in 1909-1911 to 110 in 1949-1951, the corresponding increase in rates for those 65 and over was 194 to 435 (Malzberg, 1967).

After more than 100 years of continuous increase, the number of persons resident in the state hospitals has declined every year since 1955. This has reflected the tremendous difference in resources and utilization developed since that time—especially inpatient psychiatric services in general hospitals and community mental health centers, and outpatient services in all settings. But the treatment of the aged is again quite different from that of the rest of the population. While the number of patient care episodes for the total population in all psychiatric facilities increased during the period 1966-1971 from a rate of 1,433 per 100,000 to 1,967, a gain of 37 percent, the rate for persons 65 and over *declined* 21 percent (Redick, 1973).

If the aged mentally ill are dropping out of the formal mental health services system, what is happening to them? The site of custodial care has now shifted to the nursing home. These institutions have expanded enormously, with the number of residents doubling in the years from 1963 to 1973, and resulting in a total of over 1.2 million beds. Redick (1974), in comparing mental hospitals and nursing homes, noted that in 1963, 53 percent of the aged mentally ill were in nursing homes; by 1969 the proportion has reached 75 percent. As far as the aged are concerned, the irony of the great changes in patterns of mental health care since World War I is that it has paradoxically resulted in a new, and worse, custodialism, in which the personnel and programs have even less psychological training and orientation than previously.

The deterioration in meeting the mental health needs of old people cannot be attributed simply to the pervading indifference to the aged by the mental health establishment. Among those clinicians who *do* work with the aged, it is a common stereotype that those who *don't* have psychological problems such as ". . . unresolved conflict with parental images and of the need to deny our own mortality. . ." (Lawton and Gottesman, 1974). There is no basis, however, for such naive notions assuming the superior mental health of gerontologists. This sort of *ad hominem* viewpoint actually represents a grave disservice to the aged, interfering with more cogent theoretical analysis of the factors involved in mental health systems. Since human beings will always have parents and will always die, the prospects for the aged would be rather hopeless if they had to wait for resolution of the attendant psychological problems.

It has been suggested (Kahn, 1975) that the poor mental health treatment of the aged is due to the persistent influence of the ideology of custodialism. The purpose of this chapter is to focus on empirical and theoretical issues that will reveal the manifestations of custodialism, and to evaluate the direction of future changes with more hope for the aged.

MINIMAL EXPECTATIONS: THE FOUNDATION OF CUSTODIALISM

One basic condition that permits the manifestation of custodialism is a generally negative or minimal expectation toward the mental health problems of older people. Since the aged obviously have suffered from neglect in the past, there seems to be an attitude that anything is better than nothing, and meaningless clichés substitute for demonstrable effects. The directors of some of the worst institutions proudly proclaim, "Our people come here to live and not to die." To make such a statement, surrounded by a horror of moribund aged, physically and mentally deteriorated, stewing in their own excrement, would indicate pathological lying or a psychotic delusion unless one realized that it was not to be taken literally, but had symbolic meaning only, indicating that one was to be congratulated for being at all involved with old people.

A prominent manifestation of minimal expectations is trivialization, in which the effect of a given program is so vague, nonspecific, or superficial that it is of questionable significance. This is especially characteristic of institutional settings where the level of care is so wretched that the introduction of some of the simple amenities of everyday noninstitutional living is hailed as a mental health contribution. Thus, McClanahan and Risley (1973) decided that nursing home patients should have the right to make personal choices in shopping and arranged to have a store opened in the lobby for one hour a week. The store was heavily advertised by signs and public address announcements. Research personnel recorded at three minute intervals the number and names of all patients who entered the lobby during the store period and made observations during the same time period on the other days of the week when the store was closed. They concluded that making shopping activity available resulted in substantial increases in the number of patients who were attending and participating at any moment.

Besides demonstrating methodological overkill, this study exemplifies the tautological nature of many intervention programs. The essence of the tautological study is that the outcome variable is an intrinsic redefinition of the intervention variable. This is common in programs where the intervention variable is "milieu therapy" in which additional staff are added to a unit, and the outcome variable is "increased group interaction." Perhaps the most frequent tautology is the study in which placement or discharge rate is a dependent variable, but the intervention included adding a social worker whose job it is to place patients.

In reviewing intervention programs within institutions, Lieberman (1969) feels that *any* change introduced will lead to some sort of nominal improvement, because of a "Hawthorne" effect in which any alteration in a boring and repetitive situation may lead to increased behavioral output. A breakdown in the heating system of a particularly bad nursing home has been observed to lead the usually withdrawn and isolated patients to huddle together for warmth, and, thus, to a general increase in "social interaction" (Kahn and Zarit, 1974). In this instance, an additional negative stimulus resulted in the same kind of "improvement" reported with more benevolent planned changes.

The combination of trivialization and the Hawthorne effect has produced a rash of faddish treatments exemplified by such names as "remotivation," "reality orientation," and "reality therapy" (Barns,

Sack, and Shore, 1973). These programs are characterized by increasing the stimulation and attention paid to patients and may produce some nonspecific trivial Hawthorne effect response. Staff are likely to feel much better about administering these programs because they are at least doing something, but from the patient's viewpoint they do not appear to have any substantial effect, since they are typically applied in settings and at times when custodialism has already been dominant.

LACK OF DIFFERENTIATION

One of the most astonishing manifestations of the custodial orientation and the generally low level of expectation for the aged can be found in the global, undifferentiated definition of the target "geriatric" population, particularly in institutional studies. Typical of these studies is the label "geriatric patient," in which the program population is defined solely by chronological age or by age plus the fact that the population is administratively defined by being located on a "geriatric ward." But elemental consideration of such areas as the history of mental hospitals and the relation of mental disorder to the life cycle would suggest that these populations completely distort the meaning of "geriatric." They are, in fact, largely made up of patients with congenital or other early life disorders such as mental retardation, alcoholism, and schizophrenia who have been hospitalized for many years and happened to grow old in the institution. When they reached the magic age of 65, they were transferred by the custodial institution from the adult to the geriatric wards, as if their age now made an important difference in their treatment.

Grouping diverse patients according to chronological age alone is an example of the stereotyping characteristic that Butler (1969) has called "ageism." The patients who have grown old in the hospital represent the most difficult patients to treat in the mental health system. The combination of severe, chronic illness and long duration of hospitalization, cutting the patient off from his family and any possible normal community contacts, has created some of the most hard core difficult patients. Classification of these patients as "geriatric" reflects the negative expectations for old people in general and is likely to create an atmosphere obscuring the actually good prognosis of many patients with acute disorders occurring in old age. But professionals blithely accept the population of these wards as "geriatric." Since the majority are actually chronic, untreatable patients, such programs are inevitably doomed to failure or minimal outcomes at best.

Segregation of patients by age not only reflects negative stereotypes, it in itself contributes to the custodial effect. Kahana and Kahana (1970) studied the impact of age segregation by comparing randomly assigned male admissions to a state hospital to either an age-segregated ward with only aged patients or an age-integrated ward that included the whole adult range. Each patient was evaluated for interaction in the areas of affect, responsiveness to the environment, and mental status by means of interviews, naturalistic observations, and staff ratings. Retesting was done after three weeks, which was the outer limit of the hospital system's tolerance of the random assignments. They found that patients placed in the age-integrated custodial ward and in the therapy ward showed significantly greater improvement in responsiveness and mental status than those in the age-segregated custodial ward.

Several factors are considered to have contributed to the results differentiating the age-integrated and age-segregated wards. Even though both were custodial, the integrated ward provided different role models because of having younger patients. There was more general activity, more visiting, more hope, and more planning to leave the hospital. Two social workers were assigned to this ward, while the age-segregated ward obtained social service aid only upon special request. Contrary to the expectations of some that the older persons would suffer from the activity and demands of the younger patients, they, in fact, benefited from special privileges. Younger patients offered their superior physical and intellectual resources in a nonreciprocating friendship pattern, walking the older men to meals, showers, and the canteen and allowing them to spend time outside the ward because a younger patient was watching. The older persons were given such privileges as being allowed to go to the front of the food line and to take afternoon naps, and aids were more tolerant of incontinence, even passing it off as an accident. The services of the half time physician, being less in demand by the younger patients, were more readily available to the aged patients. Finally, on the age-integrated ward, the aged developed a group cohesion and would help some of their feeble contemporaries, while on the age-segregated ward they seemed to have lost "even the identity of an old person."

THE HARMFUL EFFECTS
OF INTERVENTION

Representing more than a problem of omission, or failing to provide possible positive intervention procedures, custodial treatment may have harmful effects, adding to the psychopathology.

This view has been developed by Gruenberg (1967, 1969) in his description and analysis of the "social-breakdown syndrome." He differentiates two types of symptoms in psychoses: those that are the direct consequences of mental disorder, and those that are secondary complications due to our harmful response to the primary disorder. It is the latter, characterized by such behavior as withdrawal, self-neglect, and dangerous behavior, that he terms the social-breakdown syndrome and that form the basis for such stereotyped designations as "incapable of caring for himself" or "dangerous to self and others." Gruenberg describes a series of pathogenic steps in the evolution of this syndrome, such as labeling and extrusion, which confirms the individual's belief that he is "not quite right;" relieving him of responsibility in an overly sheltering hospital environment; and compelling isolation by cutting him off from his family ties, and compliance by learning the hospital rules and, finally, by identification with his fellow patients and by acquiring their sick role of decreasing ability to carry out ordinary social exchanges and work tasks.

Gruenberg describes these patterns of disordered social functioning as occurring independently of the particular type of mental disorder (1967). He believes that clinical evidence indicates that they are preventable by maximizing the patient's responsibility for himself and by positive expectations, but that once developed it is more difficult to reverse the process.

The recognition that there is a distinction between the primary mental disorder and the symptoms resulting from our management procedures must be considered one of the central issues in considering mental health programs for the aged. Failure to be aware of this distinction can lead to confusion of cause and effect in evaluating mental status and type of care needed. Thus, a mentally deteriorated resident of an institution will be characterized as so impaired that he requires total institutionalization when it was the institutionalization that fostered the deterioration in the first place.

Many intervention programs are really efforts to deal with the secondary symptoms, so that our therapeutic efforts can be characterized as attempts to ameliorate the very conditions we have created by our custodialist management in the first place. One of the common characteristics of institutionalized aged is that their level of functioning is poorer than would be warranted by their physical condition alone. This phenomenon has been termed "excess disability" (Kahn, 1971) and is characteristic of both self-care and cognitive functioning. A person may have all the component physiological capacities yet be unable to feed or bathe himself. Cognitively, the person may show "unorientation" (Kahn, 1971), a state in which the cognitive impairment is selectively worse in areas that have a more personal or emotional significance. The person may know the date or even the name of the president of the United States but be unable to state where he is, even after a long period of residence.

THERAPEUTIC ATTEMPTS IN CUSTODIAL SETTINGS

Some of the most ambitious intrainstitutional intervention programs have been designed just to overcome this discrepancy between potential and actual functioning. Such an attempt to rehabilitate long term nursing home patients was undertaken by a cooperative group of leaders in rehabilitation medicine and public health in New York City (Kelman, 1962). They employed matched samples of randomly assigned aged patients, compared before and after one year of intervention, with change criteria consisting of levels of function in ambulation, dressing, feeding, care of toilet needs, and transfer skills. An individually planned therapeutic program for each patient was devised, with one experimental group treated by a comprehensive rehabilitation team in the nursing home and the other transferred to an established rehabilitation hospital.

Their results showed no difference between the experimental and control groups and no significant change within any group. All groups contained some patients who improved and some who got worse, with most remaining the same. Despite employing unusually extensive and capable resources, the modest goals of the intervention were not realized. The author's explanation of these results indicates the pernicious effect of institutionalization. The patients, drawn from low and marginal socioeconomic groups, were apathetic and reluctant participants in the rehabilitation process. It required intense exhortation to get even a minority of the designated group to the hospital treatment centers. The rehabilitation goals of more independent self-care had little relevance to either the patients or the nursing home staff. The patients either were depressed and pessimistic about their futures, or they were ideologically opposed, feeling that they had a "right" to be cared for. The nursing home staff for their part felt that improved, but not complete, independence in patient functioning only led to greater demands on the staff's time and energy.

Another ambitious effort to overcome excess disability was undertaken in a home for the aged (Brody et al., 1971; Kleban and Brody, 1972; Kleban et al., 1971; Brody et al., 1974). Thirty-two pairs of women residents in their eighties were evaluated for individual areas of excess disability, such as mobility, personal self-care, and social and family relationships. Specific goals for each person were determined by an extensive interdisciplinary team on the basis of history, observation, and meetings with the family. The staff worked intensively with the experimental group, while the control group received the usual institutional care. Evaluations of change were made after one year by both staff personnel and outside observers who depended for their information on chart and other staff notes. Improvement was noted in both groups, but somewhat more in the experimental subjects. Nine months later, however, the groups were no longer distinguishable and both showed decline, despite the fact that they ". . . continued to receive. . . the normal high level of care of the sponsoring institution." These results are doubly damning, showing both that the normal procedures in a renowned institution for the aged led to behavioral decline, and that even additional intensive care had dubious short term effects.

MEANS AND ENDS IN PROGRAM EVALUATION

One of the major difficulties in altering the present pattern of custodialism in dealing with the aged is the confusion of means and ends. Professionals become committed to certain intervention methods or approaches, which persist despite controverting evidence.

Sometimes this problem arises from commitment to a certain slogan or intervention cliché that sounds as if it must be good. Thus, the cliché "alternatives to hospitalization" has led to efforts at placing the elderly in institutions other than state mental hospitals, without realizing that the alternatives, such as nursing homes, might be even worse. Epstein and Simon (1968), for example, found that they were able to effectively screen elderly patients in the San Francisco area so that none had to be sent to a state hospital. But when they compared the patients sent to a state hospital with those placed in nursing homes it was found that the latter were much more impaired in the capacity for self-care. Yet Epstein and Simon concluded ". . . that for elderly mental patients there are alternatives to hospitalization in a state mental hospital." If placement is regarded as the evaluation criterion, then their study was a complete success. If the actual functioning of the patient is the evaluation criterion, then their intervention was shown to be harmful.

In another example of intervention failure (Brody et al., 1974) in a population of residents of a home for the aged, it was explicitly suggested that a program be judged as successful not by the outcome but by virtue of the fact that the given intervention activities were performed.

This confusion of means and ends is widespread. I call it the "last paragraph phenomenon," indicating that, no matter how negative the results of a specific study, there is always a last paragraph to the effect that *despite* these results this kind of program must be continued. This point has also been emphasized by Freeman and Sherwood (1966) and by Sherwood (1972) to the effect that evaluation must be appraised in terms of outcome or program impact rather than in terms of the quality of procedures used.

This failure to appreciate the significance of negative results, even one's own, makes a mockery of the often-cited cliché of the need to get the researchers or practitioners together so that research findings can be translated into practice. Obviously, evaluation of intervention programs depends, more than on its scientific value, on value judgments (Mild, 1974) and on the impact of social and political forces (Klerman, 1974). This is a pervasive professional problem. In summarizing the review of 540 publications on memory and verbal learning for an *Annual Review of Psychology*, Tulving and Madigan (1970) concluded that: "Whenever the results of an experiment clearly do not support the hypothesis derived from a theory, the last thing the typical experimenter does is to question the theory. He usually finds good reasons why the theory should emerge unscathed from the contact with the data."

THE FUTURE

Relating this phenomenon back to the geriatric problem, it is depressing to consider that data alone is not sufficient to induce change in custodial mental health practices. Fortunately, the inertia in the system is not total, so that there have been many advances in the care of the aged aimed at minimizing or preventing some of the more gross custodial arrangements. Taking many forms—such as home care or day care, work, and educational opportunities—and employing such principles as guaranteed commitment to a defined community and minimal intervention, it has been possible to help older persons without the infantilization, extreme dependency, lack of autonomy and mobility, and loss of self-esteem characteristic of custodialism. Perhaps the fundamental changes in program orientation will come about mainly by virtue of social changes in the elderly themselves. By the year 2000, the average person aged 65 and over will have at least a high school education. Considering the impact of the large reduction in numbers of foreign born and the economic support of social security and pension systems, the aged are less likely to tolerate the indignities of custodial care.

REFERENCES

Barns, E.K.; Sack, A.; and Shore, H. Guidelines to treatment approaches: modalitics and methods for use with the aged. *The Gerontologist*, 1973, *13:* 513-27.

Brody, E.M.; Kleban, M.H.; Lawton, M.P.; and Moss, M. A longitudinal look at excess disabilities in the mentally impaired aged. *Journal of Gerontology*, 1974, *29*: 79-84.

Brody, E.M.; Kleban, M.M.; Lawton, M.P.; and Silverman, H.A. Excess disabilities of mentally impaired aged: impact of individualized treatment. *The Gerontologist*, 1971, *11*: 124-32.

Butler, R.N. Ageism: another form of bigotry. *The Gerontologist*, 1969, *9*: 243-46.

Davis, A.E.; Dinitz, S.; and Pasamanick, B. Schizophrenics in the new custodial community: five years after the experiment. Columbus: Ohio State University Press, 1974.

Epstein, L.J. and Simon, A. Alternatives to state hospitalization for the geriatric mentally ill. *American Journal of Psychiatry*, 1968, *124*: 955-61.

Freeman, H.E. and Sherwood, C.C. Research in large scale intervention programs. *Journal of Social Issues*, 1966, *21*: 11-28.

Gruenberg, E.M. The social breakdown syndrome—some origins. *American Journal of Psychiatry*, 1967, *123*: 481-89.

Gruenberg, E.M. From practice to theory: community mental health services and the nature of psychoses. *The Lancet*, 1969, pp. 721-24.

Kahana, E. and Kahana, B. Therapeutic potential of age integration: effects of age integrated hospital environments on elderly psychiatric patients. *Archives of General Psychiatry*, 1970, *23*: 20-29.

Kahn, R.L. The mental health system and the future aged. *The Gerontologist*, 1975, *15*, no. 1, pt. II: 24-31.

——. Psychological aspects of aging. In I. Rossman, ed., *Clinical Geriatrics*. Philadelphia: J.B. Lippincott Co., 1971.

Kahn, R.L. and Zarit, S.H. Evaluation of mental health programs for the aged. In P.O. Davidson, F.W. Clark, and L.A. Hammerlynck, eds., *Evaluation of behavioral programs*. Champaign, Ill.: Research Press, 1974.

Kelman, H.R. An experiment in the rehabilitation of nursing home patients. *Public Health Reports*, Public Health Service, U.S. Department of Health, Education and Welfare, 1962, *77*: 356-66.

Kleban, M.M. and Brody, E.M. Prediction of improvement in mentally-impaired aged: personality ratings by social workers. *Journal of Gerontology*, 1972, *27*: 69-76.

Kleban, M.M.; Brody, E.M.; and Lawton, M.P. Personality traits in the mentally impaired aged and their relationship to improvements in current functioning. *The Gerontologist*, 1971, *11*: 134-40.

Klerman, G. Current evaluation research on mental health services. *American Journal of Psychiatry*, 1974, *131*: 783–87.

Lawton, M.P. and Gottesman, L.E. Psychological services to the elderly. *American Psychologist*, 1974, *29*: 689–93.

Lieberman, M.A. Institutionalization of the aged: effects on behavior. *Journal of Gerontology*, 1969, *24*: 330–40.

Malzberg, B. *Mental disease in New York State 1910–1960: A study of incidence*. Albany: Research Foundation for Mental Hygiene, Inc., 1967.

McClanahan, L.E. and Risley, T.R. A store for nursing home residents. *Nursing Homes*, 1973, *29*: 10–11.

Mild, M.B. The politics of evaluation of social programs. *Social Work*, 1974, *19*: 448–55.

Redick, R.W. Patient care episodes in psychiatric services, United States 1971. Statistical Note 92. Rockville, Md.: Biometry Branch, National Institute of Mental Health, August 1973.

———. Patterns in use of nursing homes by the aged mentally ill. Statistical Note 107. Rockville, Md.: Biometry Branch, National Institute of Mental Health, June 1974.

Sherwood, S. Social science and action research. In D.P. Kent, R. Kastenbaum, and S. Sherwood, eds., *Research planning and action for the elderly: the power and potential of social sciences*, pp. 70–96. New York: Behavioral Publications, Inc., 1972.

Tulving, E. and Madigan, S.A. Memory and verbal learning. In P.H. Mussen, ed., *Annual Review of Psychology*, vol. 21, pp. 437–84. Palo Alto, Calif.: Annual Reviews, Inc., 1970.

Chapter 3

A Behavioral Approach to Geriatrics

Joseph R. Cautela
Boston College
and
Linda Mansfield
Boston College

Until fairly recently, psychological intervention has not been focused to any great extent on the behavioral problems of the elderly. Even with the new trend in research toward developing a "psychology of the aged," only a few reports have dealt directly with procedures for behavioral intervention involving geriatric populations (Butler and Lewis, 1973; Cautela, 1966b, 1966c, 1969a; Gottesman, Quarterman, and Cohen, 1973; Lindsley, 1964). One reason for this apparent lack of involvement may be related to the belief that geriatric populations generally do not respond well to treatment based on examination of their earlier experiences in an attempt to get at underlying causes of the present behavior. This type of treatment is characterized by the assumption that in order to change the present problematic behavior(s), the "unconscious" must in some manner be altered. Methods of treatment based on this model require much investment of time over long periods, and this extended treatment does not lend itself to the elderly person who may not have a great deal of time to expend in such ventures. In addition, the therapist may feel that his time and efforts are being wasted if the client is likely to die in a few years anyway.

Another obstacle to direct therapeutic intervention with the elderly relates to the influence of organic processes that occur throughout the continuum of developmental levels. A great deal of research and speculation has been concerned with the relationship between the changes in organic processes in old age (one end of the developmental continuum) and behavior. While investigation of early developmental levels has focused on the effects of the development of new capacities in a person's interaction with the environment, studies of the aged have focused on the effect of the supposed deterioration of capabilities on behavior, while at the same time minimizing environmental variables. It has become common practice to use diagnostic labels that involve organic pathology or deterioration as explanatory concepts to account for behavioral processes in the aged. One still sees this all too frequently in case histories of the aged in private and institutional settings in discussing problematic behaviors and apparent behavioral deficits in the aged. These behaviors are explained by labels such as senility, arteriosclerosis, or brain damage, or as "due to old age," and, once the label is assigned, virtually no attempt to change the behavior is made.

A current treatment modality that offers an approach for actively dealing with problems of the aged or aging is the behavioral model. The behavioral approach focuses primarily on the behaviors targeted for change and on the environmental variables that are presently maintaining these behaviors. Within this framework, diagnosis (behavioral analysis) consists of operationalizing the behaviors to be modified—e.g., depression. Once the behavior is defined operationally, the present antecedants (i.e., stimuli that trigger the problem behavior) and consequences (i.e., reinforcement, punishment, extinction) to that behavior are determined and a treatment strategy is devised. The antecedants and consequences are then manipulated.

One obvious advantage of this model is that time is not unnecessarily spent on determining the relevance of long past experiences as underlying causes of the present behavior. The present behavior itself is the target for change, and the focus of therapy is present, immediate intervention. Second, it has been noted that most older persons, when compared with younger ones, profit most from supportive approaches in which the therapist plays a more active role (Rechtschaffen, 1959). A consideration of this observation indicates that behavior therapy should achieve a measure of success with the aged. Therapy based on learning emphasizes active participation of the patient and direct intervention by the therapist, and usually involves fewer therapeutic sessions to achieve the same results as would be obtained with other modes of traditional therapy. Also, if one believes that, as an individual ages, there is a tendency toward a more primitive level of cognitive functioning, conditioning therapy would seem especially applicable.

Another factor that seems to make behavior therapy especially suitable for treatment of the aged is the observation made by a number of investigators (Freeman, 1965; Kuhlen, 1959; Oberleder,

1966) that the stress of old age is apt to be accompanied by a high level of anxiety. Reciprocal inhibition techniques, which were constructed primarily to work on the anxiety component of maladaptive behavior, would seem especially appropriate in the reduction of anxiety levels (Cautela, 1966a; Wolpe, 1958, 1969).

Another important consideration in the use of behavior therapy in geriatrics is that, in the behavioral analysis procedure, no attempt is made to use negative diagnostic labels such as senility, arteriosclerosis, and/or organic brain damage. In the behavioral model, the procedures can often be applied in a similar manner to any behavior, whether or not an organic etiology is known or implied. For example, it makes little or no difference to the behavior modifier who is trying to develop speech in a mute individual whether the individual is diagnosed as autistic, schizophrenic, brain damaged, or, as is often the case, some combination of the three. The same shaping or modeling procedures are used to develop speech regardless of the proposed organic etiology. Of course, there are some exceptions to this, such as not having Broca's area intact. Another example involves successful attempts to modify seizure behavior in individuals who have known organic pathology as determined by neurological tests (Cautela and Flannery, 1973; Forster, 1969; Gardner, 1967; Parrino, 1971; Zlutnick, 1972; Zlutnick, Mayville and Moffat, 1975). In working with seizures, the behavior therapist first identifies the antecedants that trigger the seizures. Consequences that might reinforce the seizure are also determined. The antecedants and consequences are then manipulated. One individual may be desensitized to certain stimuli that may trigger the seizure; for another individual, significant others may have to be trained to ignore the seizure in order to extinguish it.

While it is known that organic deficits do influence behavior, it does not follow that treatment has to be focused mainly on changing related behaviors by electric shock, drugs, or some other direct method such as surgery. It can be of practical and heuristic value to assume that many behaviors can at least be modified somewhat by applying specific behavior therapy procedures regardless of past history or organic involvement.

Finally, a current emphasis in behavior therapy is the notion of self-control (Cautela, 1969b; Davison and Wilson, 1975; Thorensen and Mahoney, 1974; Watson and Tharp, 1972). Self-control procedures focus on teaching an individual methods by which he can change his own behavior. The individual is taught how to do a behavioral analysis, how to identify antecedants and consequences, and how to implement change procedures. Within this framework, the change agent is the individual himself; he does indeed have an active role in shaping and controlling his environment. In regard to old age, Butler and Lewis (1973) have stated that useful "personality traits . . . are a sense of self-esteem, candor, ability to relate easily with others, independence and self-motivation, and a sense of usefulness." These are, in fact, some of the categories of behaviors that self-control procedures are intended to teach the individual.

Frequently, in old age, a person is confronted with a sense of limited capabilities in controlling the immediate environment and typically perceives himself as being a passive victim of the environment. In other words, problems are viewed as being external and uncontrollable. Teaching the elderly person methods of self-control increases his feelings of control over his environment as well as decreasing the probability of his developing new maladaptive behaviors, and this sense of mastery in turn leads to increased feelings of self-worth. The ability to manage life problems and to effectively deal with the environment are critical variables in the elderly person's perception of his own dignity as a human being.

The following presentation is a discussion of behavioral techniques for use with geriatric populations. Examples of the use of these techniques with sample problematic behaviors are also presented. It should be remembered that these techniques are usually not taught alone, but as a total self-control package.

BEHAVIOR THERAPY PROCEDURES

Reciprocal Inhibition Techniques
The principle of reciprocal inhibition states that "if a response inhibiting anxiety can be made to occur in the presence of anxiety-evoking stimuli, it will weaken the bond between these stimuli and the anxiety" (Wolpe, 1973).

Relaxation.   A response that is antagonistic to anxiety is calmness or the feeling of relaxation. The technique, taught in a manner similar to Jacobson (1938), can be effectively used by the elderly as a self-control procedure.

Geriatric clients usually take longer to learn to relax (five to ten sessions) in comparison with the younger clients (three to five sessions). The clients are taught to tighten and then loosen their muscles so that they can learn to identify the muscles that are tense in any situation. At an initial session of relaxation, elderly clients often complain of discomfort while trying to tense their muscles.

Once they have tried the technique, however, they often report that they enjoy tensing their muscles because they like the feeling of relaxing them.

After they learn to relax with ease in just a few seconds, they are instructed to relax themselves before entering a situation that they know is likely to be anxiety-provoking—e.g., meeting relatives for the first time in years. They are instructed to relax immediately if they are in a situation that is producing anxiety—e.g., being interviewed for a new job or being rejected by relatives. They are also told that, if they have just been in a situation that has produced anxiety, they are to relax afterwards—e.g., after making a mistake in counting change, they should then relax. Each step in the instructions is carefully planned and spelled out for the individual. Once they have mastery over this technique, elderly clients usually report that a great deal of happiness results from having a procedure that helps them to control their behavior.

Systematic Desensitization. In this procedure, the client is first taught to relax. A hierarchy is then constructed according to the degree of anxiety elicited by different aspects of the fear-provoking stimulus. These stimuli are presented (the least anxiety-inducing items first) to the individual in imagination until the thought of the stimulus no longer leads to an anxiety response. Direct transfer usually occurs from the imagined situation (which is accompanied by a calm response) in the therapist's office to the real life situation.

With the desensitization technique, geriatric clients have trouble retaining the scenes for any appreciable length of time. As a result, it is necessary to present shorter scenes. For example, instead of presenting this scene:

You are walking into the living room. All your grandchildren and cousins are seated around talking. You walk in, sit down near one of your grandchildren, and start to play with him.

it would be fragmented as follows:

You are walking into the living room.

When the client reports no anxiety with this scene, he can be told the following:

You notice that all your grandchildren and cousins are sitting around talking.

Gradually the client can be given the entire scene.

Another difficulty involves clarity of imagery. Usually greater detail must be presented in setting the scene. For example, if the scene concerns a confrontation with a particular individual, descriptions of his clothing, facial expressions, etc., should be provided in greater detail than is necessary with younger clients. Actual sensory decline may be the causal factor for the greater lack of clarity.

One of the most prevalent maladaptive behaviors to be dealt with in an aged individual involves feelings of rejection. This problem is especially difficult to handle because there is usually some objective reality attached to these feelings. This can be readily seen in a study by Cautela and Kastenbaum (1967) using college students as subjects; "old men" and "old women" were reported to be less preferred than "babies," "children," and "dogs." Another study done with juvenile offenders and a Catholic school population shows even less preference for the elderly by these subjects as compared with the college subjects (Cautela, Kastenbaum and Wincze, 1972).

To desensitize a person to feelings of rejection, a hierarchy is constructed concerning the individual who is supposedly doing the rejecting. For example, the client may react with more anxiety when his daughter is rejecting him than when his son is. Another hierarchy may be constructed concerning the content of the feelings. For example, some clients feel more rejected if the remarks involve their intellectual abilities rather than their physical appearance.

The usual number of presentations of the same scene in a younger client is two or three. In the elderly individual, from three to five scenes of each item are required before the client signals complete lack of tension or anxiety. Also, there appears to be more spontaneous recovery to scenes presented in the previous session. If a scene of the previous session was reported to be non-anxiety-producing at the end of the therapeutic session, during the next session that same scene may product some feelings of anxiety, even though diminished, in the elderly person. In view of this, it is recommended that the items of the previous therapy session be repeated. This usually proceeds quite rapidly. The greater problem of spontaneous recovery is easily predicted from Pavlovian theory (Cautela, 1966c).

Examples of other hierarchies that may have to be constructed are fear of heart failure, sense of personal loss due to the death of a loved one, and forced retirement.

Assertive Training. There are some very anxious clients, who seem pulled, pushed, and manipulated by individuals around them. They are often quite passive and silent when they should be assertive regarding injustices done to them. They are told in assertive training that they have to learn to speak up when they feel people are taking advantage of them and when they feel there is an injustice being done. Behavior rehearsals are conducted in the office, teaching the client how to be assertive. Being assertive reciprocally inhibits (reduces) anxiety, and of course there is the secondary reward of getting one's way. After anxious clients are able to assert themselves, there is noticeable reduction in their overall anxiety level. Also, these assertive behaviors will probably result in the achievement of some gains and an increase of respect for themselves by others and by themselves.

Two types of elderly clients need assertive training. One type is the person who has successfully retired with a great deal of money or who is still working after age 65 with power, money, and prestige. This type tends to be overassertive or aggressive. He is not often seen in the clinic, but frequently appears in private practice. He has to be taught assertive responses only in appropriate situations. Behavioral rehearsals are usually necessary. The second type of client is one who is completely dependent upon others for social and financial needs. He often feels that he is suffering many injustices, yet he is afraid to be assertive because of possible loss of those social and financial supports. He is given training in appropriate situations. One has to be very careful with this type of client because often the people who are supporting him are looking for some excuse to sever relations with him. Many behavioral rehearsals are necessary, and careful monitoring of the client's behavior is done each week as a result of the client's own reports.

When an elderly client needs training to make appropriate assertive responses, it is often evident from his history that some assertive training was necessary in his earlier years. The new adjustments required of a person after age 65 tend to exacerbate inappropriate assertive behavior. The individual mentioned above who has power and wealth, which allowed him to be relatively free from punishment in his earlier years, has lost some status because of his advanced age. Also, his sons and daughters have now grown in age and maturity so they feel confident enough to ignore or ridicule his assertive behavior. The aged individual who tended to be underassertive in his early years also now has more to lose because of fear of rejection.

Thought Stopping. Covert processes, such as particular thoughts, elicit anxiety and can be precursors to overt maladaptive behavior. Thoughts that are apt to occur in the elderly are concerned with rejection ("nobody wants me"), isolation ("I'm all alone"), and despair about the future ("I don't have much longer to live; anyway, there's not much to live for").

Thought stopping is an effective procedure for eliminating un-

desirable thoughts of elderly clients. The client is asked to close his
eyes and imagine the disturbing thought. For example, if the disturbing thought is, "I'm not useful any more," the client is instructed in
the following manner: "Now I want you to deliberately think of the
disturbing thought, 'I'm not useful any more.' Close your eyes and
think of the thought. As soon as you start thinking the thought,
signal me by raising your right index finger." When the client signals,
the therapist yells, "Stop!" in a loud voice. The usual reaction indicates a startle response. The therapist then says, "You were startled,
weren't you?" After the client answers in the affirmative, the therapist asks, "What happened to that thought I asked you to have when
I yelled 'Stop!'? The thought was displaced, wasn't it? For that one
moment, you didn't think the thought." The client always indicates
agreement concerning the blocking of the undesirable thought. Then
the therapist says, "Naturally, you can't think of two things at once.
You can't think of 'Stop' and some other thought at the same time.
Now let's try that again." After the trial is repeated, the therapist
tells the client that this time he is to again deliberately think of the
thought with his eyes closed, but he is to yell "Stop!" to himself as
soon as he starts to think the thought. When the client has done this,
the therapist asks the client if the thought went away and if he could
hear himself say "Stop" distinctly. If the client responds that he had
trouble hearing himself say "Stop," he is given a few more trials in
which he is told to say "Stop" out loud and then to imagine saying
"Stop" until he is able to report that he gets good auditory imagery
on the word "Stop." Once he is able to achieve good auditory
imagery, trials are alternated in which, on one trial, the therapist
yells "Stop" and, on the next trial, the client is to yell "Stop" to
himself when he is deliberately thinking the disturbing thought. The
client is then instructed to say "Stop" whenever he starts to think
the undesirable thought at any time outside the therapeutic situation. From then on, at weekly sessions, he is asked how much he
uses thought stopping and how effective it has been. The answers to
his questions fall into one of three categories:

1. "I use it and it is very effective. Every time, the thought went
   away. I actually started to think the thought less."
2. "I used it a lot and it worked when I was saying it, but the
   thought came back. So sometimes I got discouraged and did not
   say 'Stop.' "

If the client responds to this category, he is told to be patient. He is
told that even if he has to say "Stop" a lot for the present, usually

the thought will occur less and less. And even if this is not the case, it is better to think the word "Stop" than the undesirable thought.

3. "It worked when I used it, but many times I didn't think of saying it."

The client in this category is told, "Well, as in many other situations, it takes practice to build up a habit. So try hard in the future, whenever you think the undesirable thought, to say 'Stop.'" The client is then given ten trials in the office in which he deliberately thinks the thought and the therapist yells "Stop."

Anecdotally, thought stopping appears to be effective in reducing the frequency and duration of derogatory thoughts directed toward oneself, thoughts of despair, and thoughts considered anxiety-provoking by the client. The following is an illustration of how thought stopping was used in the treatment of an elderly female. The client lived alone and reported that many times during the day when she was alone, or sometimes during the evening, she felt a voice was telling her what to do and what not to do. She said, for example, that she would try to read something and the voice would say, "Don't do that, stop reading." If she continued reading, the voice continued. If she was cleaning the house, the voice would sometimes say, "Don't clean like that. You're not doing it right. Do it over again." Voices also disrupted her, often causing her much consternation, while she was getting dressed to go out. The voices would usually tell her that her dress didn't look good, that her dress was dirty, that her hair was messy. Sometimes it would take her two hours to dress before going out. The client was told that the voices she heard were really the result of talking to herself, probably because she was lonely in the house and the voices were a source of some companionship. In the therapy session, she was told to deliberately think the undesirable thoughts that would occur while she was doing different things. Thought stopping was taught as indicated above. The next week she reported that she had used the thought stopping technique and it was effective. The time to dress took less than the previous week. It took less time to do her housework and she was now able to read a magazine once in a while without interruption. This treatment was continued for three weeks, and at this time she reported no undesirable thoughts.

Caution: If we assume that the voices were related to some type of sensory or social isolation, then it is important to supply some sensory or social stimulation if the unwanted thoughts are to be taken away. With this client, it was arranged to have her move back to her old neighborhood, where she had many friends and easy access to public transportation. Of course, the thought-stopping procedure itself did result in sensory stimulation, but, as the frequency of the undesirable thought decreased, so did the need to say "Stop."

The efficacy of thought stopping could be explained in the counterconditioning paradigm in which the thought is substituted for the covert behavior by the word "Stop" in the presence of cues that elicit that behavior. Or, one could explain it by Pavlov's notion of external inhibition. Also, it is possible to explain the decrease in undesirable thoughts conceptually as a punishment procedure.

The interesting observations concerning the use of thought-stopping with the aged involves their reactions when the therapist yells "Stop" in the office. The elderly client seems to have a greater startle reaction and he doesn't seem to adapt easily or quickly to shouts of "Stop" in the office. Perhaps for this reason, thought stopping seems to be more effective with this population than with younger clients.

Covert Conditioning Procedures

Covert conditioning is a set of procedures in which both the response to be modified and the consequences are presented in imagination (Cautela, 1967, 1970a, 1970b, 1971, 1973).

Covert Sensitization.   In covert sensitization, the response to be decreased is paired with a noxious stimulus, and both are presented in imagination. Following training in relaxation similar to desensitization, the client is given the rationale that the present problematic behavior is a learned habit and that one way to eliminate the maladaptive behavior is to associate that behavior with an unpleasant stimulus. He is also told that this technique has been found to be effective with a variety of problematic behaviors (Ashem and Donner, 1968; Barlow, Leitenberg and Agras, 1969; Blanchard, Libert and Young, 1973; Cautela, 1970c, 1970d; Janda and Rimm, 1972; Maletzky, 1974; Sachs and Ingram, 1972). The client is then asked to imagine the response to be decreased—e.g., excessive drinking. When he can visualize engaging in the maladaptive behavior, he is asked to signal by raising his right index finger. After he signals, he is instructed in the following manner:

Now, I would like you to imagine that you decide you are going to have a drink. As soon as you make this decision, you begin to feel a little nauseous. You think, "it's nothing," and start to pour yourself a drink. As you do, you really feel like you're going to be sick and vomit. You begin to feel dizzy, and the queazy feeling in your stomach is getting worse. You pour yourself a drink anyway, but the feeling keeps getting worse. Small particles of food and vomit come into your mouth and you taste the bitter, acidy taste. You swallow it back down and raise the glass of liquor to your lips. As you do, you can't hold back the vomit any longer. Green smelly vomit pours from your mouth and nose. The acidy taste burns your mouth. The vomit goes all over your hands and clothes, and sprays on the people near you. They are disgusted, and you run out of the room embarrassed. As soon as you leave the room, you begin to feel much better.

This scene is then alternated with a scene in which the client is instructed in the same way except that he decides not to take a drink, and he immediately begins to feel much better and is calm and relaxed.

After the client signals that he is experiencing as directed, he is given five more trials of vomiting and feeling ill, and five trials of not taking the drink and feeling calm and relaxed. Usually, the vomiting trials are alternated with the calm trials. After the session, he is told to practice this procedure at least once a day at home. He is to be very careful that the vomiting or sickness occurs as he is just about to drink, or when he has the first taste.

The elderly individual appears to be more sensitive to verbal stimuli presented during covert sensitization procedures when words like "puke" or "vomiting" or "sick" or "nausea" are used. While the scenes are being presented, they groan more and show a greater number of body movements. This treatment also seems to produce better results when compared to younger clients.

The following is an illustration of covert sensitization with a geriatric client: A 67 year old man who owned a small business was referred because he sometimes would drink for four days straight. The frequency of these episodes was increasing and his business was in jeopardy. Drinking episodes were precipitated by difficulties in his business, and also by the fact that he could not bring himself to chastise his employees when they made mistakes. Covert sensitization was used by having him imagine drinking his favorite beverage, rye whiskey, in various situations in which he would get sick and vomit. He was told that whenever he felt an urge to drink, he was to yell "Stop!" and to imagine vomiting. He was also taught relaxation and desensitization to the great tension he felt when something went wrong with the business. He was also desensitized toward difficulties in business and taught assertive behavior toward his employees. Within a few weeks, he reported that he could drink for only a day at a time. After a few more weeks, he reported that he could take one drink but didn't have to continue drinking. He was told to try not to drink at all, and covert sensitization sessions were continued.

It appears that aversive stimuli such as imagining vomiting or hearing someone yelling "Stop" seem to result in a more intense response in the geriatric population. Perhaps this results in greater modification of behavior. If this observation concerning the extra sensitivity of the elderly population to aversive stimuli is valid, then one has to be especially careful to consider the overall physical health of the patient—e.g., heart condition or gastric complications due to nausea that might be produced by covert sensitization scenes. Of course, one has to be very careful if there has been any previous trouble with physical health. In the case mentioned earlier, this was taken into consideration, as the physical condition is always a special concern in any therapeutic endeavor. However, special consideration should always be given when aversive stimuli are presented.

Covert Reinforcement.   In the application of the covert reinforcement (Cautela, 1970b) procedure the client is asked to imagine clearly the response to be increased (e.g., "No matter how bad things seem, it's still worthwhile living"). This is usually a response that is antagonistic to a negative thought. Once the client clearly imagines the thought to be increased, he is then asked to shift to a reinforcing or pleasant scene (e.g., "You are eating your favorite cake"). If the scene is actually reinforcing, then the thought will actually increase in probability of occurrence.

Experimental evidence is accumulating that indicates that covert reinforcement is effective in increasing response probability (Ascher, 1973; Cautela, Walsh, and Wish, 1971; Flannery, 1972; Krop, Calhoon, and Verrier, 1971; Wisocki, 1973). Also, thoughts such as "I am a worthwhile person" or "I can learn to enjoy myself, even though I have no friends at the moment" can be increased in a similar manner.

Removal of Fears.   Anxiety due to overt aversive stimuli such as rejection by others, fear of making mistakes, fear of ridicule, or fear of adapting to a new situation can be reduced by desensitization or by covert reinforcement. The desensitization procedure that has been described in detail elsewhere (Wolpe, 1958, 1973) can be used to eliminate all of the above-mentioned fears. However, recently covert reinforcement has been employed with some success to modify avoidance behavior (Cautela, Walsh, and Wish, 1971; Krop, Calhoon, and Verrier, 1971). Below are some examples of its application.

Fear of rejection. The elderly person who reports this fear is asked to imagine, for example, that his daughter ignores him at the dinner table, but it doesn't bother him (response to be increased), and then he is to shift to a pleasant scene (e.g., an old acquaintance telling him how good he looks).

Fear of failure. A client is asked to imagine, for example, that he tries to catch a ball and he drops it. His grandchildren laugh, but he feels calm and it doesn't bother him (response to be increased) and he switches to the reinforcing scene.

Covert Extinction. Covert extinction (Cautela, 1971) is a covert conditioning procedure in which an individual imagines he is making the response that usually gets reinforced by the environment and then he is instructed to imagine that the response is not followed by reinforcement. Many times a behavior is reinforced outside of the treatment session faster than it can be extinguished by the treatment. The usual procedure in this case is to enlist the cooperation of significant others to withhold reinforcement when the client makes the maladaptive response. For example, the elderly often express somatic complaints because of the attention they get from staff or relatives (especially since they don't get enough reinforcement whenever they're not complaining). Sometimes relatives are unable to ignore the problematic behaviors. Under these conditions, covert extinction can be most helpful.

In using covert extinction, the rationale for the procedure is first explained to the client. The client is then asked to imagine that he is making a response such as "Oh, I feel awful" or "I am getting too old." He is then instructed to imagine that no one is paying attention or responding to him in any way. Some individuals find it reinforcing to contemplate the effect their suicide will have on other people. Those reinforcing effects are identified, and then the client is asked to imagine that, after his death, the anticipated reinforcing effects do not occur.

Increasing the Probability of Reinforcers

It is important for the individual to have an adequate reinforcement menu from which he can sample because (1) lack of adequate reinforcers is itself aversive and (2) reinforcers are necessary to shape and maintain behavior.

There is some evidence that when organisms undergo extinction, aggression is elicited (Bandura, 1969). And some writers (Ferster, 1965; Lazarus,1968) are of the opinion that so-called "depressive" behaviors are the result of a meager reinforcement menu. Reinforcement loss due to a decrease in prestige or social status, and a decrease in the range of reinforcers because of reduced income are likely to occur after retirement. Reinforcement loss is, of course, more acute for individuals who do not have a source of reinforcement such as hobbies or recreation outside their vocation.

As an individual becomes older, reinforcement loss, due to departure of loved ones, is apt to increase. With declining sensory acuity, reinforcers available from reading, watching TV, listening to the radio, and eating decrease. As the individual grows older, he is less preferred as a companion as compared with other age groups (Cautela and Kastenbaum, 1967). This results in a loss of possible social reinforcers from children, relatives, and strangers. Also, as elderly people retire they usually have to rely on neighborhood relationships. When their wealth, occupation, or race differs from that of other local residents, the elderly tend to be more isolated (Rosenberg, 1968).

Providing Reinforcers

The behavioral analysis necessary for increasing the reinforcement menu for each individual includes the determination of what reinforcers are lacking and what situations are likely to act as reinforcers. The behavioral analysis includes interviews with the client and with significant others, as well as the administration of the Reinforcement Survey Schedule (Cautela and Kastenbaum, 1967). The following treatment procedures are often indicated as a result of behavioral analysis with elderly clients:

1. **Teaching the elderly to be more reinforcing to others.** Often elderly people are critical of the behaviors of their children or younger adults because they don't behave in a manner as expected by the elderly individual. Treatment consists of desensitizing the elderly individual to the behaviors he finds aversive. Also, behavioral rehearsals are held teaching the elderly individual when and how to reinforce the behavior of others. For example, one elderly individual was instructed to constantly reinforce his daughter by smiling and complimenting her whenever she did anything for him.

2. **Increasing social participation.** Covert reinforcement can be used to increase social participation by a shaping procedure. The elderly individual is asked to imagine that he has agreed to go to a party and delivers reinforcement to himself. He is next asked to imagine that he is leaving the house and again is reinforced. He is

walking toward a house for the party—reinforcement. He is then walking into a room filled with people and feels comfortable—reinforcement. At the same time, he is encouraged to actually perform the behaviors imagined in the scenes, e.g., actually calling up an old friend and asking him to the ball game. This procedure can also be employed to encourage courting behavior if the individual is so inclined.

3. Possible relocation. The decision whether to suggest relocation for the elderly individual depends on a number of variables such as which location is likely to provide maximized reinforcement, how aversive relocation is to the individual, and the attitudes of the individual toward relocation. Fear of relocation may be reduced by desensitization and covert reinforcement of appropriate behavior in a manner similar to the procedure used to increase social participation. Attitudes can also be changed with covert reinforcement (Cautela, Walsh, and Wish, 1970; Cautela and Wisocki, 1969). For example, the elderly individual is asked to make the statement to himself: "If I move to another place, I'll be much better off." Then he is to deliver reinforcement. Or perhaps he may be instructed to think: "Just because I'm going to a nursing home doesn't mean I'm being put out to pasture"—reinforcement.

4. Increasing task participation. Because of decreasing sensory acuity and decreasing reaction time, the elderly individual observes that it is more difficult to learn new tasks. Programmed teaching methods should be used since they allow the individual to proceed at his own pace and provide reinforcement at small, successive steps. Covert reinforcement procedures can be effective in increasing the individual's willingness to engage in new tasks. He can be asked to imagine that he is about to approach a task and receives reinforcement; then that he is actually engaging in the task—reinforcement; then he imagines that he is engaging in a task but makes a little mistake but feels calm—reinforcement; and so on.

5. Reinforcing behavior during the interview session. The therapist, when working with the elderly, usually has to take a more active role than in therapy with young adults. He has to reinforce the elderly individual as much as possible for every behavior no matter how small as long as it is adaptive. If the individual says that he has been going for a walk every day, then that behavior should be praised as being very constructive in terms of health, meeting new people, and so forth. Also, whenever the client makes any statement about positive self-regard, the therapist can follow it by verbal and non-verbal reinforcement.

6. **Possible vocational activity.** For some elderly individuals, it may be possible to provide for new vocational placement by vocational testing and by reducing anxiety related to a possible new job. Desensitization and covert reinforcement can be effective in reducing anxiety and increasing appropriate behavior to a new vocation. Of course, such a possible placement depends upon the health and financial conditions of the client.

7. **Instructions to significant others.** In some cases, reinforcement may be increased by instructing significant others on what behavior to reinforce in the elderly, and how to deliver the reinforcement. For example, sons and daughters may be taught to choose situations in which they can compliment and praise their mother every time she helps in any way.

AN EXAMPLE OF A BEHAVIORAL INTERVENTION: PREVENTION OF SUICIDE

There is an assumed relationship between "depressive" behaviors outlined previously and the increased probability of suicide. The model presented below concerning the etiology and prevention of suicide appears quite simplistic as contrasted with the dynamic foundations presented by various suicidologists such as Schneidman (1970). In the authors' opinion, this model has greater practical value for suicide prevention. We will concern ourselves here only with the individual who has consciously made an attempt to end his life. Other classifications of "subintentional" or "unintentional" death such as those classified by Schneidman (1970) are not considered.

The viewpoint presented here does not consider the construct of the "unconscious" or the concept of guilt as useful concepts either to explain or to prevent suicide behavior. Within a learning theory model, the following factors may combine as determining conditions for suicidal behaviors. They are:

1. aversive stimuli, e.g., as rejection by others or pain;
2. lack of adequate reinforcement; and
3. escape conditioning as a learned response.

When the above three conditions are present, suicide is always a possibility, especially if the elderly person talks about suicide. For, contrary to the report of Ravensburg and Foss (1969), Weisman (1970) warns that persons who talk about suicide should be taken seriously.

Suicide as Escape Behavior

Though aversive stimulation and lack of reinforcement are present in some individuals, attempts as suicide are not the primary behavioral response in evidence. However, other individuals are apt to respond to strong aversive stimulation and lack of adequate reinforcement by escape responses that may include suicide. These latter individuals have been conditioned (shaped) to rely on escape as a method of dealing with aversive stimulation. Suicide behavior, of course, is the ultimate escape. These individuals are apt not to consider or have available to them alternatives for removing aversive stimulation.

Conditioning to rely heavily on escape behavior to reduce anxiety can occur from a number of sources:

1. **Modeling.** Seeing significant others (e.g., parents or friends) using escape behavior may teach an individual to rely on escape behaviors.

2. **Lack of adaptiveness.** The individual might not have learned adaptive ways to handle stressful situations, and may have been used to relying on alcohol or drugs to escape from stressful situations. So when these individuals are confronted with a "no way out" situation, the thought of suicide may occur. This thought may be reinforcing— i.e., there is immediate reduction of anxiety—since the individual will (correctly) perceive that such behavior would terminate the aversive situation around him.

Experimentally, it has been shown that escape conditioning can be extinguished by removing aversive stimulation, and by providing reinforcement for incompatible behavior (Reynolds, 1968). The treatment procedures, therefore, would employ behavior therapy procedures to remove aversive stimulation and reinforce incompatible behavior. As previously discussed, removal of aversive stimulation can be accomplished with procedures such as systematic desensitization, thought stopping, relaxation, assertive training, and covert reinforcement. Amount and range of reinforcers can be increased in a number of areas such as social participation, learning new tasks, providing new locations, and changing attitudes.

GENERAL CONSIDERATIONS

A wide gamut of behavior therapy procedures can be employed in working with the elderly. Throughout the present discussion, general observations and guidelines have been discussed in terms of applying the techniques to the elderly individual. In summarizing these considerations, the following should be taken into account when teaching the elderly self-control procedures:

1. Training in relaxation may require more practice sessions in order to learn to relax well.

2. Special consideration should be given to sustaining attention during treatment sessions. In some cases, more trials may be required to ensure the effectiveness of the procedure, e.g., more and shorter desensitization trials.

3. The elderly client should frequently be questioned regarding sustaining imagery when covert procedures are employed.

4. Previous learning trials may need to be reviewed at therapy sessions to guard against spontaneous recovery of a previously extinguished response.

5. One has to be extra careful in the use of aversive procedures with the elderly due to a greater arousal response when aversive (non-pain-inducing) stimuli are presented. In addition, if at any time aversive procedures are indicated, it is recommended that covert procedures be employed as they are less likely to be as harmful as overt aversive procedures.

6. When setbacks occur in treatment, the therapist should be careful to take an active role in providing additional support and encouragement. The more past conditioning trials of a maladaptive response, the more difficult it may be to quickly modify the response. In these circumstances, the client should be reminded that it takes time to "unlearn" a habit, and that sometimes the environmental conditions can exert a great impact on his behavior at the present stage of treatment.

7. It is most important to solicit cooperation from significant others to increase the amount of reinforcement in general and to aid in removing the effects of aversive stimuli. This is usually due to the state of dependency felt by the elderly, since they are often truly dependent on the resources of others.

Behavior therapy techniques offer a wide range of possibilities in therapeutic intervention with the elderly. With the emphasis on self-control, the elderly client is given an armamentarium that he can utilize to deal more effectively with the world around him. At this stage of life, when the tendency too often is to focus on limitations, behavioral procedures can provide the elderly individual with the opportunity to work from his strengths. These procedures can provide one means by which we all can actively live out our lives with the respect and dignity deserving of every human being.

FUTURE AREAS OF RESEARCH AND SPECULATION

Certainly, much more work needs to be done in designing clinical treatment intervention programs for the elderly. Empirical investigations are sorely needed to determine the relevant parameters of treatment techniques as well as research involving relative efficacy of the procedures. Hopefully, some of the observations and speculations in this Chapter will entice some current researchers into exploring the possibilities of this kind of approach. The venture will most assuredly be reinforcing.

As a final and additional provocation, the use of behavior therapy with geriatrics also leads to such speculative questions as:

1. What are the parameters of the "will to live"? Can the "will to live" be increased through reinforcement procedures? If so, what are the ethical boundaries?
2. Can a physical environment be created in which the happiness and potential of the elderly can most effectively be maximized? What kinds of prosthetic devices and reinforcements can be utilized in accomplishing this end?
3. What are the potentials in utilizing reinforcement techniques to make dying less aversive? What kinds of procedures can be utilized and under what conditions should they be employed when working with dying behavior (both in terms of the individual who is dying and significant others)?

This is a challenging field and the challenge needs to be met.

REFERENCES

Ascher, L.M. An analog study of covert positive reinforcement. In R.D. Rubin, J.P. Brady, and J.D. Henderson, eds., *Advances in behavior therapy*, vol. 4. Proceedings of the Fifth Conference of the Association for the Advancement of Behavior Therapy. New York: Academic Press, 1973.

Ashem, B. and Donner, L. Covert sensitization with alcoholics: A controlled replication. *Behavior Research and Therapy*, 1968, *6*: 7–12.

Bandura, A. *Principles in behavior modification*, pp. 374–75. New York: Holt-Rinehart-Winston, 1969.

Barlow, D.H.; Leitenberg, H.; and Agras, W.S. The experimental control of sexual deviation through manipulation of the noxious scene in covert sensitization. *Journal of Abnormal Psychology*, 1969, *74*: 596-601.

Blanchard, E.R.; Libert, J.M.; and Young, L.D. Apneic aversion and covert sensitization in the treatment of a hydrocarbon inhalation addiction: A case study. *Journal of Behavior Therapy and Experimental Psychiatry*, 1973, *4*: 383-87.

Butler, R.N. and Lewis, M.I. *aging and mental health: positive psychosocial approaches.* St. Louis: The C.V. Mosby Co., 1973.

Cautela, J.R. A behavior therapy approach to pervasive anxiety. *Behavior Research and Therapy*, 1966a, *4*: 99-109).

————. Behavior therapy and geriatrics. *Journal of Genetic Psychology*, 1966b, *108*: 9-17.

————. The pavlovian theory of old age. *The Gerontologist*, 1966c, *6*, no. 3, pt. II: 27.

————. Covert sensitization. *Psychological Reports*, 1967, *20*: 459-68.

————. A classical conditioning approach to the development and modification of behavior in the aged. *The Gerontologist*, 1969a, *9*, no. 2, pt. I: 109-13.

————. Behavior therapy and self-control: Techniques and implications. In C. Franks, ed., *Behavior therapy: appraisal and status.* New York: McGraw-Hill, 1969b.

————. Covert negative reinforcement. *Journal of Behavior Therapy and Experimental Psychiatry*, 1970a, *1*: 273-78.

————. Covert reinforcement. *Behavior Therapy*, 1970b, *1*:33-50.

————. The use of covert sensitization in the treatment of alcoholism. *Psychotherapy: Theory, Research and Practice*, 1970c, 7: 86-90.

————. Treatment of smoking by covert sensitization. *Psychological Reports*, 1970d, *26*: 415-20.

————. Covert extinction. *Behavior Therapy*, 1971, *2*: 192-200.

————. Covert processes and behavior modification. *Journal of Nervous and Mental Disease*, 1973, *157*: 27-36.

Cautela, J.R. and Flannery, R.B., Jr. Seizures: Controlling the uncontrollable. *Journal of Rehabilitation*, 1973, *39* (3): 34+.

Cautela, J.R. and Kastenbaum, R. A reinforcement survey schedule for use in therapy, training, and research. *Psychological Reports*, 1967, *20*:1115-30.

Cautela, J.R.; Kastenbaum, R.; and Wincze, J. The use of the fear survey schedule and reinforcement survey schedule to survey possible reinforcing and aversive stimuli among juvenile offenders. *Journal of Genetic Psychology*, 1972, *121*, 255-61.

Cautela, J.R.; Walsh, K.; and Wish, P. The use of covert reinforcement in the modification of attitudes toward the mentally retarded. *Journal of Social Psychology*, 1971, *77*: 257-60.

Cautela, J.R. and Wisocki, P.A. The use of imagery in the modification of attitudes toward the elderly: A preliminary report. *Journal of Psychology*, 1969, *73*: 193-99.

Davison, G.C. and Wilson, G.T. Behavior therapy: A road to self-control. *Psychology Today*, 1975, *9* (5): 54-60.

Ferster, C.B. Classification of behavior pathology. In L. Krasner and L.P.

Ullman, eds., *Research in behavior modification*, pp. 6-26. New York: Holt-Rinehart-Winston, 1965.

Flannery, R.B. A laboratory analogue of two covert reinforcement procedures. *Journal of Behavior Therapy and Experimental Psychiatry*, 1972, *3*: 171-77.

Forster, F. Conditional reflexes and sensory-evolved epilepsy: The nature of the therapeutic process. *Conditional Reflex*, 1969, *4*: 103-14.

Freeman, J.T. Body composition in aging. In J.T. Freeman, ed., *Clinical features of the older patient*, pp. 3-43. Springfield, Ill.: Thomas, 1965.

Gardner, J. Behavior therapy treatment approach to a psychogenic seizure. *Journal of Consulting Psychology*, 1967, *31*: 209-12.

Gottesman, L.E.; Quarterman, C.E.; and Cohen, G.M. Psychosocial treatment of the aged. In C. Eisdorfer and M.P. Lawton, eds., *The psychology of adult development and aging*, pp. 378-423. Washington: D.C.: American Psychological Association, 1973.

Janda, L.H. and Rimm, D.C. Covert sensitization in the treatment of obesity. *Journal of Abnormal Psychology*, 1972, *80*: 37-42.

Jacobson, H.A. *Progressive relaxation*. Chicago: University of Chicago Press, 1938.

Krop, H.; Clahoon, B.; and Verrier, R. Modification of the "self-concept" of emotionally disturbed children by covert reinforcement. *Behavior Therapy*, 1971, *2*: 201-04.

Kuhlen, R.G. Aging and life adjustment. In J.E. Birren, ed., *Handbook of aging and the individual*, pp. 852-97. Chicago: University of Chicago Press, 1959.

Lazarus, A.A. Learning theory and the treatment of depression. *Behavior Research and Therapy*, 1968, *6*: 83-89.

Lindsley, O.R. Geriatric behavioral prosthetics. In R. Kastenbaum, ed., *New thoughts on old age*, pp. 41-60. New York: Springer Publishing Co., Inc., 1964.

Maletzky, B.M. "Assisted" covert sensitization in the treatment of exhibitionism. *Journal of Consulting and Clinical Psychology*, 1974, *42*: 34-40.

Oberleder, M. Psychotherapy with the aged: An art of the possible. *Psychotherapy: Theory, Research and Practice*, 1966, *3*: 139-42.

Parrino, J. Reduction of seizures by desensitization. *Journal of Behavior Therapy and Experimental Psychiatry*, 1971, *2*: 215-18.

Ravensburg, M.R. and Foss, A. Suicide and natural death in a state hospital population: A comparison of admission complaints, MMPI profiles, and social competence factors. *Journal of Consulting and Clinical Psychology*, 1969, pp. 466-71.

Rechtschaffen, A. Psychotherapy with geriatric patients: a review of the literature. *Journal of Gerontology*, 1959, *14*, 73-83.

Rechtschaffen, A. and Maron, L. Effect of amphetamine on sleep cycle. *Electroencephalography and Clinical Neurophysiology*, 1964, *16*: 438-45.

Reynolds, G.S. *A primer of operant conditioning*. Glenview, Ill.: Scott, Foresman and Co., 1968.

Rosenberg, G.S. Age, poverty, and isolation from friends in the urban working class. *Journal of Gerontology*, 1968, *23*: 533-38.

Sachs, L.B. and Ingram, G.L. Covert sensitization as a treatment for weight control. *Psychological Reports*, 1972, *30*: 971–74.

Schneidman, E.S. Orientations toward death. In E.S. Schneidman, N.L. Farberow, and R.E. Litman, eds., *The psychology of suicide*. New York: Science House, 1970.

Thorenson, C.E. and Mahoney, M.J. *Behavioral self-control*. New York: Holt-Rinehart-Winston, 1974.

Watson, D.L. and Tharp, R.G. *Self directed behavior: self-modification for personal adjustment*. Monterey, Cal.: Brooks/Cole, 1972.

Weisman, A.D. Project omega: Probing fatal illness and suicide. *Massachusetts General Hospital News*, 1970, *29* (1): 3–5.

Wisocki, P.A. A covert reinforcement program for the treatment of test anxiety: Brief report. *Behavior Therapy*, 1973, *4*: 264–66.

Wolpe, J. *Psychotherapy by reciprocal inhibition*. Stanford: Stanford University Press, 1958.

———. *The practice of behavior therapy*. New York: Pergamon Press, 1969.

———. *The practice of behavior therapy*. 2nd ed. New York: Pergamon Press, 1973.

Zlutnick, S.I. The control of seizures by the modification of pre-seizure behavior: the punishment of behavioral chain components. *Dissertation Abstracts International*, 1972, *33*, (6-B).

Zlutnick, S.I.; Mayville, W.J.; and Moffat, S. Behavioral control of seizure disorders: The interruption of chained behavior. In R. Katz and S. Zlutnick, eds., *Behavior therapy and health care: principles and applications*. New York: Pergamon Press, 1975.

Chapter 4

Psychodiagnostics of the Elderly

Guillermo A.A. Bernal, Linda J. Brannon,
Cynthia Belar, John Lavigne, and Roy Cameron
Duke University Medical Center

INTRODUCTION

The research literature in the field of geriatrics has provided some basic factual information about normal and
abnormal aging with respect to changes in the central
nervous system. For example, with increasing age there is a decrease
in speed, sensory efficiency, flexibility, and power to assimilate new
skills. Although some of these central nervous system (CNS) changes
are considered to be irreversible, they need not have irreversible
effects on behavior. The notion of irreversibility has affected the
interpretation of psychological tests and psychotherapeutic intervention with older patients.

The test results of older people seem to fit the stereotyped notions
of older individuals as being rigid and constricted, and as having poor
memory and many changes in personality. The clinical psychologist
in the applied setting has not been immune to the stereotyped
notions.

The responsibility of the clinician, as Oberleder (1964) states, "is
to find the response behind the response, to uncover the potential of
the aging individual which may be hidden not only from the examiner but from Subject as well." To do this the clinician may need
to make changes in the administration of psychometric tests, thereby
compensating for the CNS changes noted above, and also to be
sensitive to the older person's specific physical and emotional needs.

The clinician in the applied setting is being asked more and more
to evaluate and aid in the diagnostic process of older individuals. He

finds himself having to answer questions about intellectual functioning, personality change, and differential diagnosis between functional and organic disorders in older patients. The question is: How well is the clinician prepared for this emerging task? This chapter attempts to answer this question by reviewing some of the psychodiagnostic materials available for evaluating and diagnosing behavior in the elderly.

The first section discusses the measurement of intelligence in old age. It also reviews the course of intellectual changes and the structure of the intellect in old age. The second section is concerned with the assessment of organicity in the elderly patient. It reviews the available tests and discusses the issue of functional versus organic disorders in psychiatric patients. The third section reviews the traditional tests used in the assessment of personality and their adaptability to older persons. The final section reviews the more recently developed techniques of assessment and diagnosis for use with the aged.

ASSESSMENT OF INTELLIGENCE IN GERIATRIC PATIENTS

Introduction

In the early years of the intelligence test movement, attention was focused primarily on developing instruments for use with school-children. Recently, however, the need for assessing the intelligence of geriatric patients has been increasingly recognized. In part this is due to the fact that the geriatric population is rapidly increasing in size. In part it is also due to the utility of intelligence tests for assessing the geriatric patient's current level of functioning and for predicting his ability to function in other environments, including rehabilitation programs.

Serendipitous findings of longitudinal studies of intelligence have further indicated the importance of intelligence tests. Measures of general intellectual ability have been shown to be related to life expectancy in the elderly. Cosin, Mort, Post, Westropp, and Williams (1957) divided patients into good, moderate, or poor groups on the basis of mental and physical tests and found that a greater proportion of the patients in the poor group had died within six months. Jarvik and Falek (1963) report similar results using certain of the Wechsler Adult Intelligence Scale subtests. Kleemeier (1961, 1962) examined the aging curves of men who were given the Wechsler-Bellevue test at two year intervals for 12 years. These men were all in their sixties at the time of initial testing. Kleemeier discovered individual differences in the rate of decline in performance, with the rate of decline being more marked for men who died before the completion of the study. This finding suggests a relationship between this "terminal drop" and life expectancy.

Administration

The administration of intelligence measures to geriatric patients demands slightly different expectations and more flexibility than are appropriate when working with young or middle-aged adults. As Oberleder (1967) cautions, the examiner must be aware that the older patient may approach the test with less confidence and more apprehension than a younger patient. He may well view the test as a measure of memory and "his tenseness and thought-blocking may indeed cause temporary memory loss which will then affect his entire testing session." Because of performance anxiety, consideration should be given to not administering the intelligence test as the first measure of the assessment battery.

Numerous other factors such as fatigue, short attention span, and hearing difficulties may force changes in the normal administration of the test battery. Repeating instructions, giving the patient frequent opportunities for rest periods, and conducting the tests over multiple sessions may all be necessary. The slower response time of elderly patients demands that the examiner give the patient sufficient time to answer—more time than the examiner might allow for younger adults.

Physical limitations, too, may interfere with the nonverbal performance tasks, and in some instances it may not be possible to administer these tests. This occurred during the attempts to standardize the Wechsler Adult Intelligence Scale (WAIS) with older people (Doppelt and Wallace, 1955). Oberleder (1967) suggests that a practice period may be necessary. Although many of the above changes depart from standard procedures, they are performed in the interest of obtaining the best possible estimate of the patient's potential ability. More experimentation with such methods is clearly indicated, but is potentially very tedious for the experimenter. One such effort by Doppelt and Wallace (1955) demonstrated that timing and speed have very little effect on the aged's performance on the WAIS. It also showed that group measures of intelligence are unsuited for large segments of the geriatric population.

Issues in the Study of Intelligence in the Aged

Two critical questions about the nature of intelligence in old age are still debated and unresolved. The questions concern the course of intellectual changes in old age and the structure of intellect during that time of life.

Studies of age changes in intelligence during the middle and later years have generally utilized either longitudinal or cross-sectional methodologies, frequently with somewhat discrepant results. The earliest studies employed the cross-sectional approach and found marked decrements in performance through adulthood (e.g., Jones and Conrad, 1933; Miles and Miles, 1932). These studies demonstrated sizable declines in intellectual ability even though relatively young subjects were included in the samples. In both of the studies cited above, the ages of the subjects ranged between 20 and 50. When cross-sectional studies have been performed with older subjects, as in the WAIS standardization sample (Doppelt and Wallace, 1955), which included subjects between 60 and 74, marked declines on psychomotor tests and lesser declines on verbal tests have been reported.

The deficiencies in cross-sectional studies of age changes in intelligence have long been recognized, and the normative data on age changes they yield have been suspect. The basic critique of cross-sectional studies is that this method compares people of different ages rather than the same people at different ages. As a result, differences between people of different ages are obtained rather than age changes in the same people, and it is frequently argued that the longitudinal method is the only valid means of delineating age changes in intelligence during maturity and old age (Botwinick, 1967).

Longitudinal investigations have generally shown less severe declines in intellectual ability as a function of age. Several of these studies are reviewed in Botwinick (1967). Owens (1953), for example, reanalyzed the Jones and Conrad (1933) sample by the longitudinal method, retesting the 19 year old sample at age 49, and found increases on four of the eight scales that Jones and Conrad had reported to have declined. Another study also reports increases in intelligence until at least age 50 (Bayley and Oden, 1955).

At least two other longitudinal studies have examined age changes in older populations. Jarvik, Kallmann, and Falek (1962) retested a population of twins on three occasions and at ages above those mentioned in the previous studies—at mean ages of 67.5, 68.4, and 75.7 years. These investigators reported significant decreases on speeded psychomotor tests but not on tests requiring more verbal, symbolic, abstracting abilities. Eisdorfer (1963) retested subjects age 60 and above on the WAIS after a three year interval and found no significant changes in verbal, performance, or full scale I.Q.s. Thus, in contrast to cross-sectional studies, longitudinal studies have found either smaller decrements or no decrement at all in intellectual ability. This has prompted Eisdorder (1963) to conclude that "normative data collected by cross-sectional sampling may exaggerate the pattern of decline in old persons."

Yet longitudinal studies also contain biases that limit their usefulness for generating accurate normative data. Generally, the subjects who participate in longitudinal investigations are unusually highly motivated and cooperative, as they would have to be to participate in the repeated evaluation that longitudinal studies demand. Frequently, too, there is a sampling bias inherent in longitudinal studies whereby subjects who survive to the retesting are found to be brighter than the nonsurvivors at initial testing (Riegel, Riegel, and Myer, 1967; Savage, 1971; Savage, Britton, George, O'Connor, and Hall, 1972). This bias tends to counteract any large intellectual decline that may be noted in cross-sectional studies.

Schaie and Strother (1968a; 1968b) have proposed critiques of both methods of investigation, as well as a possible method of generating more accurate data on age changes in intelligence. These authors note that cross-sectional studies compare subjects who are of different ages and are members of different cohorts (i.e., generations). Because the subjects belong to different cohorts, there may be systematic genetic and experiential differences between the different age samples. As a result, any performance differences that emerge may be due to maturational differences between the subjects of different ages (true age differences), to cohort differences (genetic or experiential), or to both age and cohort differences. In longitudinal studies, the same subjects are tested at different times and any differences that emerge cannot be attributable to cohort effects. Differences between the performance of the subjects at the several testings, however, may be due to true age differences, or to intervening experiential factors that occur between testings (time differences), or both. The authors note that, because of the extraneous influences on performance, the cross-sectional and longitudinal study results can agree only under special circumstances; furthermore, neither one alone can be relied on to yield accurate normative data on the changes in the performances of elderly adults.

Schaie and Strother (1968a; 1968b) propose a cross-sequential design that combines elements of both the longitudinal and cross-sectional methods and that has potential for generating more accurate normative data. In this method, subjects of several ages are tested on repeated occasions, and composite longitudinal and cross-sectional gradients of performance are generated. The longitudinal curve can then be compared to the cross-sectional gradient and inferences can be made about time and cohort effects.

Schaie and Strother (1968a; 1968b) have presented data derived using this method with subjects between the ages of 21 and 75. The data suggest that (1) a major portion of the variance in cross-sections studies is attributable to cohort effects, (2) cross-sectional methods overestimate the effects of aging on intelligence for unspeeded measures of ability and underestimate its effects for highly speeded measures, and (3) longitudinal methods underestimate aging effects on unspeeded tasks and overestimate aging effects for speeded tasks. Further examination and use of this method may be useful in resolving the differences between the results of cross-sectional and longitudinal methods. The method also deserves utilization with different instruments and with older subjects than were employed in most of the studies mentioned earlier.

A second basic issue in the nature of intelligence of geriatric patients concerns the structure of intellect in the aged. Knowledge of maturational changes in the structure of intellect is incomplete and in need of organization. Several studies of the structure of intellect in old people are reviewed in Botwinick (1967) and will be summarized here. Cohen (1957) identified four factors in the 60 and over group from Doppelt and Wallace's (1955) standardization sample. These included a verbal comprehension factor, a perceptual organization factor, and a memory factor, plus one factor that was not labeled. This is one factor fewer than was found in younger age groups from the standardization sample. When the same data were reanalyzed by a different method (Berger, Bernstein, Klein, Cohen, and Lucas, 1964), the factor loadings of certain tests had changed. Birren (1952) analyzed data from subjects between ages 60 and 74, and identified factors similar to those Cohen (1957) discovered in his younger age ranges. Riegel and Riegel (1962) found no changes in the structure of intellect with age.

As Botwinick (1967) notes, coherent summaries of such data are difficult. The structures that are finally identified seem heavily influenced by initial differences in the tests administered and in the method of analysis employed. While memory seems to account for larger portions of the variance in older samples, this could be due to cohort effects as well as to true maturational changes. Furthermore, none of the studies that were located for this review examined structural differences among the subjects in the very broad age range of 60 to 80.

Measures of Intelligence

Intelligence tests that are properly standardized for geriatric populations, and therefore of clinical usefulness in assessing the individual, are surprisingly rare. Norms for the aged on many instruments that are typically used with adults are either inadequate, poorly described, or difficult to locate. For some instruments, norms were not discovered by the reviewers, or were not reported to exist in the most recent *Mental Measurements Yearbook* (Buros, 1972). The task of uncovering norms provides a serious hurdle for the clinician who wishes to interpret the intelligence test data of his geriatric patients in a meaningful way.

The Wechsler Adult Intelligence Scale (Wechsler, 1955) is familiar to all clinicians and is the most popular measure of intelligence with geriatric populations. Norms on the WAIS for subjects over 65 are presented in the test manual (Wechsler, 1955). The norms were collected on a Kansas City population by Doppelt and Wallace (1955), who felt that their sample was suitable for developing norms for the elderly. Wechsler (1955), however, correctly advised caution in the use of the norms for subjects over 65 because the norms were "not based on cases tested throughout the country according to census specifications." Studies by Eisdorfer and his colleagues (Eisdorfer, Busse, and Cohen, 1959; Eisdorfer and Cohen, 1961) lend credence to this warning. Eisdorfer et al. (1959) and Eisdorfer and Cohen (1961) compared data collected on a large sample of subjects in the Duke University area with the normative data collected from Doppelt and Wallace's (1955) Kansas City sample. There were consistent differences, with Duke project subjects of different ages, sexes, races, and economic classes consistently attaining higher mean scores on the verbal scale and lower mean scores on the performance scale than were obtained in the Kansas City standardization sample. Because of this, Eisdorfer and Cohen (1961) concluded that "the need for establishing national norms on a national sample of the aged is demonstrated."

Normative data has also been gathered for differences in performances on the WAIS verbal and performance scales in aged samples (Field, 1960). These data, however, had been gathered on the Kansas City sample and thus may also be inaccurate. In any event, the WAIS currently remains the best standardized measure of intelligence for use with the aged.

Norms for adults on the Quick Test (Ammons and Ammons, 1962), a short, verbal measure of I.Q., are also available as part of each test form. This form states that the standardization sample was "rigorously quota-controlled for age," but in fact none of the subjects were above the age of 45. Age corrections for subjects between 40 and 75 have been developed based on Wechsler's (1958) data, which shows a decline in verbal I.Q. with age, but, as the authors note, "as recognition vocabulary (the type of item included in the Quick Test) may well decline more slowly than the skills tapped by Wechsler's Verbal items, the correction procedure should be used with caution" (Ammons and Ammons, 1962).

Levine (1971) and Gendreau, Roach, and Gendreau (1973) have attempted to extend the norms for the Quick Test to the elderly. Levine's (1971) study included subjects between ages 60 and 100; Gendreau et al. (1973) included subjects with a mean age of 80. Both of these studies, however, failed to obtain the large number of subjects needed for adequate standardization; there were less than 50 subjects in each study. Furthermore, neither study systematically sampled subjects with regard to race, socioeconomic status (SES), or education. The high correlations with the WAIS (.88 with full scale I.Q.) obtained by Gendreau et al. (1973) suggest that this may be an instrument worth further attention.

Norms on a third measure of intelligence that utilized verbal measures of I.Q., the Shipley Institute of Living Scale, have been presented by Mason and Ganzler (1964). These norms were developed to provide an estimate of normal intellectual impairment in an aging sample. The data were collected on Veteran's Administration Hospital patients between the ages of 25 and 75, without regard for education, SES, or geographic sampling. All subjects, of course, were male. More adequate norms for both sexes were not located for this instrument.

Group measures of intelligence, such as the Otis Self Administered Test of Mental Abilities, and nonverbal measures of intelligence are frequently not suitable for use with geriatric subjects because of their short attention spans or physical limitations. Hence, normative data on nonlanguage measures of geriatrics are even more rare than on verbal measures of geriatrics. Such measures as the Progressive Matrices and Porteus Maze tests occasionally appear in research studies with geriatric patients, whose performance is generally poorer on these measures than that of younger adults and adolescents (Loranger and Misiak, 1960). Nonetheless, nonverbal tests with geriatric patients can occasionally be useful, for example, in the testing of deaf patients.

Raven (1965) has presented normative data for the Progressive Matrices Test in the form of percentile rankings for subjects between the ages of 60 and 80. Raven acknowledges the difficulty of assuring an adequate cross-sectional representation of the geriatric population in Great Britain (or anywhere). His standardization sample includes only healthy subjects from one community center in Great Britain. A representative selection of subjects of different races, socioeconomic status, educational background, and geographical areas was not secured.

While many of the standard clinical instruments are unquestionably in need of upgraded norms, even newer tests are being developed. One of these, the Geriatric Interpersonal Evaluation Scale (GIES; Plutchik, Conte, and Lieberman, 1971), is a brief battery that is intended to be a screening device for evaluating the cognitive and perceptual functioning of geriatric patients. Another instrument has been developed by Williams (1970) and is composed of material drawn from the Wechsler-Bellevue, the Wechsler Memory Scale, the Progressive Matrices, and other instruments. Validity data for these instruments either are not available or are difficult to locate at this time.

ASSESSMENT OF ORGANICITY IN GERIATRIC PATIENTS

In this section, an attempt will be made to review some of the tests currently used in clinical situations to assess organic impairment in geriatric patients. The applicability of specific tests will be evaluated with respect to their utility in differentiating brain-damaged elderly patients from their normal peers, as well as from functionally impaired groups in the same age range. Some issues relevant to this area of psychodiagnosis will also be mentioned.

Tests for the Assessment of Organicity in Geriatric Patients

Although the WAIS and Wechsler-Bellevue tests are often cited as being useful for determining localization of impairment in subjects of all ages, there is evidence in the literature that a discrepancy in verbal scale and performance scale scores may be quite misleading when observed in elderly subjects. In an article on the effects of past experience on test performance in the elderly, Williams (1960) found that elderly subjects showing large difference between verbal and performance type tasks were fairly numerous. In these cases, the subjects' scores clearly reflected occupation, training, or hobbies in earlier life. Williams notes that those individuals who spent their lives working with their hands and utilizing perceptual data retained the ability to deal with perceptual and constructional problems, while they performed poorly on tests requiring verbal skills. She cautions: "Before it is possible to generalize about an older person's intelligence or intellectual deterioration from his performance on tests, it is clearly necessary to take into account his past life as well as present condition."

Several of the tests in the Halstead Neuropsychological Battery seem to hold considerable promise for clinical application with aging patients, although age-appropriate norms for elderly subjects are not currently available. Reitan (1959) compared the effects of brain damage on the Halstead Impairment Index and certain variables from the Wechsler-Bellevue Scale using subjects with a mean age of about 32. (The Impairment Index was a composite score based on ten "discriminating" tests in the Halstead Battery). He reports that this index is significantly more sensitive to brain damage than any of the Wechsler-Bellevue variables selected, including verbal I.Q., performance I.Q., full scale I.Q., Wechsler Deterioration Quotient, "hold" tests, and "don't hold" tests. It must be emphasized that these findings hold only for the age group sampled. The applicability of these results for elderly patients depends upon replication of the above findings, taking into account relevant age norms. The need for normative data on the elderly is highlighted by Reitan's (1955b) finding that non-brain-damaged subjects begin scoring within the brain-damaged range on the Halstead Impairment Index at age 45–50. It is of little consolation to the clinician who must diagnose organicity with available but inappropriate norms to know that it is only when brain damage is clearly present that age per se will not significantly affect this index (Reitan, 1955b).

Reitan's Trail Making Test (TMT), one of the scales included in the Halstead Impairment Index, has been used alone as an index of brain damage (Reitan, 1955a). In a study examining the effects of age and of brain damage on TMT performance, Davies (1968) found that the diagnostic significance of the test depended in part on the ages of the samples used. Thus, when normal subjects in their sixties and seventies were tested, from 76 to 92 percent of those investigated scored within the brain-damaged range according to Reitan's cut-off scores. Clearly, if the TMT is to have diagnostic value with old patients, an allowance for age must be made in locating a cutting point for organic impairment.

The Mental Status Questionnaire (MSQ) developed by Kahn, Goldfarb, Pollack, and Peck (1960) has been widely used clinically as a brief objective measure that the authors consider valid "for the determination of mental status in the aged, particularly for disorders associated with cerebral damage." Consisting of ten questions designed to assess orientation and general information, the MSQ requires little time to administer and allows objectivity and uniformity of observations across different examiners. Kahn et al. demonstrated that in a sample of 1,077 geriatric patients, 94 percent of those who made no errors on this test were classified by psychiatrists as "none" or "mild" organic brain syndrome (OBS), while 95 percent of those making ten errors, were rated as moderately or severely organic. The MSQ was also found to be highly related to evaluation of presence of psychosis associated with OBS and degree of patient management problems. Markson and Levitz (1973) modified the MSQ items, and used a scalogram technique of analyzing MSQ responses to develop a Guttman scale to assess memory loss among the elderly. The authors report the advantages of this modification to be that (1) the items tap "a single dimension of memory loss believed to be associated with organic impairment rather than either several dimensions of memory loss or lack of information on a given topic. . .", and (2) the score obtained reveals what items were answered incorrectly. This MSQ modification was also demonstrated to be significantly predictive of mortality; in a sample of 254 geriatric patients, 23 percent of low scorers had died after one year versus only 3 percent of high scorers. In fact, memory loss was a more accurate predictor of mortality than the ADL (a measure of ability to perform activities of daily living) and patients' self-assessment of overall health.

Inglis (1959) developed for use with elderly psychiatric patients a paired associate learning test that he reports is sensitive to memory impairment. However, subsequent work (Newcombe and Steinberg, 1964; Irving, Robinson, and McAdam, 1970) suggests that, while this test may significantly discriminate between functional and organic patients, the percentage of misclassification is too high to justify its use as a clinical diagnostic instrument. Another test of short term verbal memory, the Modified Word Learning Test (MWLT), was not found by Newcombe and Steinberg (1964) to significantly discriminate organic patients from functional patients in an aged psychiatric population (n=22). However, Bolton, Savage, and Roth's (1967) research with 144 geriatric patients found that organic patients scored significantly lower on the MWLT than did groups diagnosed as schizophrenic, affective disorder, and normal. These authors found that, excluding patients with focal lesions, they could classify 80 percent of the sample correctly (including 100 percent of the normals), and that those misclassifications that did occur resulted in part from less intelligent nonorganic subjects obtaining high organic scores. They conclude that the MWLT is a "more useful diagnostic test of generalized brain damage than the deterioration indices and verbal performance discrepancy scores calculated from the WAIS," but caution clinicians against drawing conclusions from test results obtained from aged subjects with low I.Q.s.

The Memory for Designs (MFD) test is a test of visual memory that has been widely used to assess organicity in patients of varying ages. However, Payne's review (Buros, 1972) notes special problems inherent in using the MFD with aged populations. More recent norms gathered on 240 English subjects, broken down by sex and age decade (20-80), reveal that the normal age decline on this test is greater than suggested in the previous norms. Thus, if the original norms are used in interpreting test scores of older subjects, a number of false positives may result. Payne also criticizes the lack of norms for psychiatric groups, stating that at present the possibility of psychiatric disorder cannot be ruled out as an alternative explanation for a low MFD score (a criticism substantiated by Newcombe and Steinberg's [1964] research in which the MFD failed to discriminate between organic and functional aged psychiatric patients).

The Wechsler Memory Scale is another test used frequently in assessment of impairment in memory function. Wechsler's manual (1945) provides score corrections for age groups ranging from 20-24 years through 60-64 years of age. The means of Memory Scale subtests for two age groups of normal subjects reported in the manual clearly reflect a drop in performance on all subtests as early as age 40-49, when overall I.Q. is held constant. In spite of this evidence that performance in normals deteriorates with age, neither score corrections nor normative data are currently available for use with individuals over 64, a group in which assessment of memory function is often critical to evaluation of organic impairment.

Arthur Benton's Revised Visual Retention Test is often used for assessment of visual perception, visual memory, and visuoconstructive skill in clinical cases where organic brain damage is suspected. The 1963 edition of the manual for the *Revised Visual Retention Test* reports that there is a significant relationship between Visual Retention Test performance and chronological age, such that performance level on this test shows a progressive rise from age eight until a plateau is reached at ages 14-15 and maintained through the thirties. "A decline in efficiency of performance occurs in the forties and this decline is progressive, continuing through the successive decades of life." Benton also reports on an unpublished study by von Kerejarto (1963) of 50 normal subjects aged 65-75. Interpretation of an individual's performance on the Benton is based on a calculated "number correct" score that is compared to an expected score for his age range, as well as a calculated "error" score that is also compared to an expected error score. In this study, the mean "number correct" score was found to be three points below the expected "error" score for the younger subjects. Nonetheless, Benton's norms for adults offer a correction factor only for subjects up to age 64 years, both for "number correct" score and for "error" score. An obtained "number correct" score that is three points below the expected score is considered to "suggest impairment," and an obtained "error" score which is five or more points above that expected is considered a "strong indication" of impairment in functioning, despite the fact that these figures represent mean scores for at least one sample of normal elderly subjects. Again, further normative data is needed to establish the value of this test for use with elderly patients.

The Hooper Visual Organization Test (VOT) was specifically devised as a test for diagnosing organic brain pathology and for differentiating organic from functional and motivational disorders. Although the VOT has been demonstrated to have useful validity in differentiating organic patients from those with functional disorders in a VA Hospital population (Hooper, 1952), its applicability to elderly patients may be limited without further standardization on aging subjects. (The norms collected by Mason and Ganzler [1964] involved only male VA patients.) In an unpublished study (Hooper, 1948) reported in the VOT manual, a group of residents from a voluntary home for the aged (mean age 76.8 years) was given the VOT. A significant negative correlation ($r = -.57$) between age and VOT score was obtained. Using a VOT cutting score of 20, 67 percent of the group were diagnosed as having organic brain pathology with moderate impairment, 15 percent with mild impairment, and 18 percent with no impairment. Hooper (1958) states that "these results seem consistent with the known effects of aging on brain structure." However, it must be determined from additional research whether 82 percent is an accurate figure for the incidence of organic brain pathology in the nonhospitalized population that was sampled.

One test for assessment of organicity that deserves special attention is the Face-Hand test (Fink, Green, and Bender, 1952). This test has wide applicability in that it is a culture-free, unlearned perceptual task that can also be used with non-English-speaking populations. It involves ten trials of touching the patient simultaneously on the cheek and dorsum of the hand. Patients with organic dysfunction frequently report only one of the two stimuli, or displace the source of one stimulus (usually hand to face). Fink et al. noted that, by the tenth trial, 87 percent of the brain-damaged patients continued to make errors, whereas less than 0.5 percent of normals and less than 3 percent of schizophrenics continued to make errors. Later research by Kahn, Goldfarb, Pollack, and Peck (1960) involving 1,077 geriatric patients demonstrated that 70 percent of those patients with negative test results were classified as none or mild OBS (psychiatric diagnosis), while only 27 percent of those with significant test results were diagnosed as none or mild OBS. Although these percentages reflect a rather high miss rate, the authors did demonstrate test results to be highly related to psychiatrists' evaluations of presence of psychosis associated with OBS and degree of patient management problems. Irving, Robinson, and McAdam (1970) subsequently found the Face-Hand test to be a significant discriminator between functional and organic aged psychiatric patients (92 percent of functional and 76 percent of organics were correctly identified), and conclude that this test is valid enough for clinical application, especially if used in combination with other psychometric data.

One of the most commonly used perceptual-motor tests for assessing organic dysfunction is the Bender Gestalt. Although Oberleder (1967) states that the Hain (1964) scoring method "for identifying brain damage in older people has recently been developed," it is noted that Hain's original validation groups had mean ages of approximately 47 years (brain-damaged) and 35 years (psychiatric), and that in his cross-validation sample the average age was approximately 55 years and 50 years for brain-damaged and psychiatric groups respectively. These are hardly geriatric samples that permit establishment of norms specific to the aged population. In addition, it was noted in the original validation sample that age was significantly positively correlated with the Bender score (i.e., older subjects made more errors suggestive of CNS dysfunction), although the amount of variance accounted for by age was less than 10 percent. Hain did demonstrate, however, that his scoring method could differentiate organically impaired individuals from functional psychiatric patients, although false negatives (especially in patients with focal lesions and seizure conditions) were more frequent than false positives. The Background Interference Procedure (BIP) developed by Canter (1966) has been demonstrated to increase the sensitivity of the Bender Gestalt in discriminating organic from non-brain-damaged psychiatric patients. However, it is noted that his validation samples included 151 subjects, of whom only 15 were over the age of 60 years, and that no standard is provided with which to compare the performance of the elderly with the rest of the population.

Critical Issues

In the preceding discussion of tests used for assessing organicity in the aged population, reference has frequently been made to the validity of the test in discriminating between functional and organic disorders in psychiatric patients. This differential diagnosis is perhaps the most frequent one that the clinical psychologist is called upon to make in his contact with geriatric patients.

Although data suggest that the Bender Gestalt and BIP may be helpful in making this diagnosis in adult populations (Hain, 1964; Canter, 1966), the lack of norms available for the geriatric population (which may "normally" perform at a lower level) makes their utility in answering this diagnostic question suspect for the aged. As previously stated, the lack of normative memory for design data on psychiatric patients makes this test inappropriate for use in this differential diagnosis in any age group. Research is also reported that does not support the use of the WAIS vocabulary and digit span scores in differentiating between functional and organic geriatric patients (Roth and Hopkins, 1953; Hopkins and Roth, 1953). Even the WAIS verbal-performance discrepancy and WAIS deterioration quotient are reported to be invalid in classifying geriatric patients into categories of neurotic, normal, psychotic, or organic (Bolton, Britton, and Savage, 1966). However, these authors do provide data to which the clinician can refer in order to evaluate the significance of an obtained index with respect both to age group and to probability of such a discrepancy in a given population.

Newcombe and Steinberg (1964) found a delayed recall task to be the most helpful memory test in differentiating organic from functional disorders in a geriatric sample. Organics manifested severe retention deficits, even with practice, whereas the functional group demonstrated cumulative learning. In addition, data do exist on geriatric population that support the use of an information test constructed by Roth and Hopkins (1953), the Modified Word Learning Test (Bolton, Savage, and Roth, 1967; Riddell, 1962), Ravens Progressive Matrices, the Face-Hand test, a names learning test, and an orientation test as described by Irving et al. (1970) in differentiating between organic and functional aged psychiatric patients. (Readers should refer to the Irving et al. article to obtain the cut-off scores that yielded maximum discrimination by the last four tests.) However, misclassifications do occur, which these authors attribute to (1) the inefficiency of the measures, (2) errors in diagnostic criteria, and (3) the fact that differences in extensiveness and localization of brain damage result in varying behavioral manifestations. They conclude that combinations of tests would have greater validity and therefore more utility in distinguishing between functional and organic disorders than do single measures.

As Williams (1970) points out, however, most of the research in this area has differentiated *groups* in which the clinical diagnosis was clear-cut. The psychologist in the clinic is frequently presented with individual cases in which the data are equivocal and a diagnosis cannot be made on the basis of already available information (physical findings, electroencephlographic (EEG) findings, history). Williams states that in such cases "the diagnosis often has to be based on qualitative rather than quantitative aspects of behavior and the test is used as a standard situation to elicit signs rather than as a measuring device." An excellent summary of these differentiating signs with respect to emotional expression, psychomotor behavior, verbalizations, orientation, and perception is provided by Williams (1970). Also provided is a list of qualitative signs that may be helpful in differentiating between focal and generalized cerebral lesions, an important discrimination in terms of implications for treatment and prognosis.

Another issue frequently referred to in the preceding discussion has been the need for appropriate norms in assessing organicity in the geriatric population. It has been repeatedly demonstrated that increased age is associated with lower levels of functioning on psychometric tests, even in non-brain-damaged samples (Reitan, 1962). Granick and Friedman (1967) point to the need for considering education and age as variables in establishing geriatric norms, demonstrating that the negative correlation of education with age is a significant factor in the decline in performance noted on psychological tests. In their research, performance on 27 out of 33 tests was shown to decline with age, although with the effects of education taken into account, only 19 of these tests reflected a decline in performance.

Clearly the clinical psychologist must be aware of the influence of factors such as education, overall intellectual level, and test-taking attitudes, and of the lack of appropriate norms in evaluating the performance of geriatric patients on tests of organicity. Given that the relevant age norms do not at present exist, however, it is essential that the clinician attend to qualitative aspects of performance as well as obtain information about the patient's level of functioning in daily living in order to appropriately evaluate mental integrity.

PERSONALITY EVALUATION OF OLDER INDIVIDUALS

Introduction

It seems that controlled studies of the personality changes that occur in older individuals are very rare despite the fact that our aging population is on the increase. Clinical psychologists for the most part appear to have concentrated on defining symptoms and measuring their changes as the individual grows older. There is a lack of reliable norms for older individuals in our current diagnostic techniques. The projective tests are perhaps the ones that are the most lacking in this respect. It is clear that many of our traditional projective tests do not lend themselves to the specific but diverse problems of old people. Some of their problems are isolation, loss of physical mobility, decrease in physical and sexual attractiveness, social prejudice, change in their dependency status, and more practical issues such as poor health, finances, and housing.

The most commonly used tests to assess personality are the Rorschach, the Minnesota Multiphasic Personality Inventory (MMPI), and the Thematic Appreciation Test (TAT). This section will review some of the literature on these tests and discuss their adaptability for use with an aged population.

The Rorschach

As early as 1942, Rorchach in his book *Psychodiagnostics* set forth the hypothesis that old people tend to become slower, less productive, and less efficient. Their "thought content seems restricted with an apparent instinctive regression to a more infantile level" (Klopfer, 1946). Klopfer confirmed Rorschach (1942) in his work with 50 subjects 60 years and older. He concluded that the trend for older individuals is one of constriction, a decrease in the number of responses, a decrease in the number of human figures and movement, an increase in animal responses, and a decline in form level rating.

Klopfer's (1946) findings seem to have been supported in the literature. Prados and Fried (1947) worked with 35 normal old adults ranging in age from 50 and 80 and concluded that as individuals grow older there is a significant decrease in their creative and intellectual powers. In support of Klopfer's (1946) findings, Chesnow, Wasika, and Reinitz (1949) and Grossman, Worshawsky, and Hertz (1951) all conclude that older persons have perceptual difficulties and show a paucity of responses, emotional constriction, unclear forms, and a general decrease in the level of functioning.

One of the very few large scale studies of older persons' performance on the Rorschach, that of Ames, Learned, Metraux, and Walker (1954), seems to have serious methodological flaws and has limited application for the clinician in an applied setting. Ames et al. analyzed the responses of 200 men and women between the ages of 70 and 100; of these individuals, one third were institutionalized. Ames et al. interpreted test behavior in terms of test theory in a circular fashion. These investigators used the Rorschach performance itself as a criterion for adjustment. They classified their subjects into three groups (normal, preseniles, and seniles), based on a comparison of their responses and the response found in the protocols of children. Ames (1960) states that "in many respects the changes which take place with increasing age seems to be the reverse of changes which take place between childhood and adulthood".

Oberleder (1967) strongly criticizes Ames et al. for what she calls "test bound reasoning," which she believes not only preserves stereotypes but also tends to overlook alternative interpretation to the results obtained. A study by Light and Amick (1956) with 50 non-institutionalized subjects pointed to the importance of using normal subjects with an independent measure of intellectual performance available for such subjects if the Rorschach data are to be used as normative standards.

Eisdorfer (1963) examined the WAIS and Rorschach records of 242 older individuals between the ages of 60 and 94. This study will be reviewed in detail because it illustrates the type of research needed in this area. Eisdorfer divided his subjects into four age categories, 60–64, 65–69, 70–74, and 80+. He also divided them into three groups according to their full scale WAIS I.Q. scores, group 1 (low I.Q., below 85), group 2 (average I.A., 85–115), and group 3 (high I.Q., above 116).

Eisdorfer's results do not support some of Klopfer's (1946) conclusions about the Rorschach performance of old people. Klopfer's conclusion that the fraction of whole response (W percent) decreased in old age was not supported by Eisdorfer. His study shows the W percent ranged from a low of 32.6 for subjects ages 75–79 with average I.Q., to a high of 55.6 for subjects ages 60–64 with a high I.Q.

Eisdorfer's data only partially support Klopfer's conclusion of a paucity of responses (R) with increasing age. The below average I.Q. groups in Eisdorfer's study showed an almost linear decrement for subject R with increasing age, while the average I.Q. groups showed only a tendency. There was no evidence of any age-related decline in the high I.Q. group.

This study also does not support the view that older individuals have a low rate of large details (D percent). Eisdorfer found no consistent pattern of change with age and no consistent effect within age and intelligence.

His study found that the perception of human movement (M) was related to intelligence, with the low and average I.Q. groups showing a decline in M with age, while the high I.Q. groups showed an increase.

The reliance on Form (*F* percent) and Color (*C*) as determinants did not show any age change, but was directly related to intelligence, with the low and average I..Q. groups relying the most on form and using the least color.

In terms of content, Eisdorfer's study found that the number of Popular (*P*) responses was fairly constant with age. The percentage of animal (*A*) responses showed an increase for the low and average I.Q. groups but not for the high I.Q. groups. The average and below average groups produced very few human responses (*H*), in contrast to the high I.Q. groups.

The importance of Eisdorfer's study for the practicing clinician is that it can be seen as a baseline measure for the interpretation of the Rorschach in older individuals. His conclusion is that what in the past have been thought to be pathological signs of aging may be artifacts of institutionalization or of the I.Q. of the older individual.

Adaptability of the Rorschach to an
Older Population

Oberleder (1964, 1967) has been one of the most vocal critics of the use and adaptation of current psychological techniques in the testing of the aging. She offers alternative interpretation of the constriction, paucity of responses, increased animal action, and fewer human responses found in the Rorschach protocols of older individuals.

Oberleder states that the constriction observed in older persons may reflect excessive caution or a fear of risk that results in excessive concern with accuracy and what may be a safe response. She cites Geerstman (1962), who carried out a factor analysis of Rorschach scoring categories and found a "perceptual accuracy factor" that his young normal subjects used to avoid the risk of revealing themselves in this situation. The records of these young subjects were similar to those of older individuals.

Another alternative that Oberleder suggests is that the Rorschach inkblots may be too ambiguous a stimulus to evoke a response in view of the fact that older people have a more heightened need or arousal than do younger subjects.

Other signs of constricted, superficial reactions to the Rorschach, such as poor form, few responses, and increased animal action, may reflect a self-imposed avoidance of dangerous stimulations. In addition, the increased number of animal responses of the aged may give us an idea of their inner motivations. Older individuals seem to substitute animal action for human action as a means of expressing their inner feelings. Oberleder points out that their poor form may reflect not poor ego control or reality contact, but rather, a detachment from a rejecting, uncaring environment.

The Eisdorfer (1963) study and the comments of Oberleder (1964, 1967) indicate that it is inappropriate to try to apply the norms for other age groups in interpreting the Rorschach of older people. They also indicate the need for more studies with normal population, like that of Eisdorfer, in other areas of the country to establish baseline data for adequate interpretation of the Rorschach protocols of the aged.

The Minnesota Multiphasic Personality Inventory (MMPI)

The MMPI is probably the most widely used inventory of personality by clinical psychologists. However, there seem to be few reported studies in a normal aged population.

Hathaway and McKinley (1951) do not comment in the revised edition of their *Minnesota Multiphasic Inventory Manual* on the effects of age on test results except to say that the test may be administered to any individual over 16 years of age.

The early studies of Brozek (1955), Aaronson (1958, 1960), and Calden and Hokanson (1959) all seem to indicate that aged individuals have higher elevations on the Hs and Hy scales and on the Si scale than do younger adults. They also seem to suggest that there is a lowering of the character disorder and psychotic scales of the MMPI. The only problem with these studies is that they do not deal specifically with those who are considered older individuals, approximately 60 and above, so that they cannot be used as normative data.

Swenson (1961) administered the MMPI group test to 95 normal subjects more than 60 years old, 31 men and 64 women. Swenson's results, like those of the previous invetigators, indicate that older individuals tend to score higher on the neurotic triad and on the social introversion (Si) scale, and low on the remaining scales, with Pd and Ma scales being the lowest. However, Swenson does not statistically evaluate the data, thus making it difficult to compare it with that of other researchers.

Postema and Schell (1967) analyzed and compared the data of Swenson's study with their data on 34 subjects aged 60 and 22 younger psychiatric patients. They compared their subjects on a neurotic index (scales Hs, D, and Hy) and on a psychotic index (scales Pa, Pt, Sc, and Ma). Their results confirm the results other investigations: older normal individuals tend to endorse more neurotic views than the MMPI standardization group (young adults). They do not differ from this group in the extent to which they agree with psychotic like views. The effects of both age and psychopathology seem to be reflected in the fact that older psychiatric patients tend to agree more with neurotic than psychotic views, but they are also more prone to agree with either view than are either the MMPI standardization group or normal old people.

Kornetsky (1963) administered the individual card form of the MMPI to 43 normal subjects ranging in age from 65 to 91 years old, and with a mean I.Q. of 110. He, like other investigators, found significant elevations on the neurotic triad and Mf. He suggested that the elevation of Mf may be due to intelligence and educational factors.

Gynther and Shimkunas (1966) reported on the MMPI and the WAIS scores of 420 hospitalized psychiatric patients, ranging in age from 14 to 76 (mean age 35). The patient I.Q.s range was from 59 to 137 with a mean of 98. Their results indicate that the scales affected by age were Pd, Pa, Sc, and Ma, with older subjects scoring lower on all of these than younger patients. Scales L and F were affected by intelligence, with scale F affected by both variables. The D scale T-score was not affected by age, but a study of the peaks showed that most older patients tend to have scale D peaks. Gynther and Shimkunas conclude that their data do not support the implications of previous studies that as individuals grow older they admit to more dysphoric behavior. Instead, they suggest that a better interpretation may be that, for psychiatric patients at least, there is less admission of rebelious and impulsive behavior with increasing age.

Britton and Savage (1965) administered the full card form of the MMPI to 83 female and male normal subjects aged 70 and above. They found that the subjects showed significant deviations on all scales except for Pd and Si. They also reported that the means of the K, D, and Sc scales are raised by more than one standard deviation. They suggest that investigators refrain from applying the standard normative MMPI data to aged subjects.

Adaptability of the MMPI to an Aged Population

The MMPI is a long and tedious test for an older person, whose attention span is generally short, who may have visual difficulties, and whose physical strength in general may be low. The usual self-administration of the MMPI is also ill suited for older persons. The administration suggested by some of the other studies reviewed above may be more appropriate. Several studies use the individual card form, which can be either read or presented one at a time to the subject and marked by the examiner. This technique avoids any confusion with the answer sheet and the marking of the appropriate space on it. Attempts should also be made at standardizing a shorter version of the MMPI, such as the Mini-Mult (Kincannon, 1968) or the Faschingbauer (1974) abbreviated MMPI (FAM), for the aged population.

When interpreting the profile of an older person, the multiple social and psychological aspects confronting him must be kept in mind. In addition to the usual difficulties encountered by the young, the aging also bring with them problems unique to their group. The older patient is faced with the imminence of death. He is usually depressed, or bordering on this condition. His memory in certain areas has begun to fail, his relationships with others have changed, and he finds himself less attractive than before. Each aspect of old age mentioned above has a place in the evaluation of the older individual's MMPI.

The Thematic Apperception Test (TAT)

A new projective technique specifically designed for older people, the Gerontological Apperception Test (GAT) will be discussed in this section. The GAT is based on the TAT and uses themes and situations that are congruent with those found in the elderly and that are not usually found in a younger population. The figures portrayed in the GAT are those of older individuals, so as to ease identification of the patient with the test stimuli.

The GAT consists of 14 cards in which scenes frequently encountered by old people are depicted. The instructions are similar to those of the TAT. They require the subject not just to describe the picture, but to tell a story about each card. The subject must give his story a beginning, a middle, and an ending.

The authors of the GAT (Wolk and Wolk, 1972) state that it can be given as part of a test battery and that all or select cards from the GAT may be used. The authors also suggest that the GAT be used for screening purposes prior to individual and group psychotherapy with older patients.

So far there seem to be no research studies dealing with the applicability and validity of this test. However, its development is important because it highlights the necessity for custommade projective techniques for the elderly or adaptation of older existing ones.

ECOLOGICAL ASSESSMENT: A NONTRADITIONAL TREND IN GERIATRIC EVALUATION

"Judging from the current state of the ·clinical field outside gerontology . . . the standard psychodiagnostic battery has declined in its centrality to the role of the clinician." In gerontological psychology, this is not necessarily a bad thing, if we could develop in its place a truly *ecological* approach to assessment. That is, the assessment task is to determine what an older person can do, given a particular situation or a choice of situations. The situation is an equal partner with intraindividual factors in determining the adequacy of behavior. Thus, in rehabilitation, milieu therapy, or screening and placement, the clinician should be asked to choose dimensions of functioning, and tasks with which to measure them, that are relevant to the older person's environment (Lawton, 1970a). There is a great need to develop a technology of choosing relevant areas to test, finding the right testing techniques, and helping the older person and those who are in a position to help him to plan and function in an environment most congruent with his capacities. Frequently it will be more useful to test the individuals' ability to perform concrete tasks of daily living, rather than the unearthing of unconscious wishes or the detailing of a psychodynamic personality sketch" (Lawton, 1970a). The following discussion is a overview of ecologically oriented assessment procedures that are specifically related to geriatric populations.

In the past decade or so, clinicians and researchers have become increasingly aware of the need to assess the elder person's functioning as directly as possible. In commenting on the significance of functional assessment in clinical evaluation, Katz, Downs, Cash, and Grotz (1970) noted that "emphasis on function has practical importance, since function can be measured relatively objectively, is a measurable milestone in the course of illness, and is sensitive to changes of illness and aging. Functional status also reflects the existence, stage, and impact of unfavorable forces at a time when knowledge about cause and pathogensis is not advanced enough to permit measurement in the latter terms. Measures of function, thus, become useful indicators of severity and of the changing course of illness and aging." As such, measures of function are invaluable for purposes of dispositional decisionmaking (a sense of the patient's functioning is clearly necessary if the dispositional decision involves selection of a new environment for him to ensure congruence between patient functioning and environmental demands) and used in a pre-post followup design for evaluation of clinical programs.

Attempts have been made to develop behavioral rating scales that refer to objective behaviors and reflect the elderly patient's level of functioning in quantified form. Although a host of scales of this sort have been developed, many remain unpublished and/or have not be extensively studied or widely used. The present discussion will focus upon scales that have been described and documented in published reports. Many of the other existing scales tend to be developed for use in specific studies in particular institutions. (Most notably, investigators at the Philadelphia Geriatric Center have developed and adopted a number of interesting assessment scales that will potentially be of interest to the reader. See, for example, Lawton's 1972 article.)

Relatively simple rating scales that assess disability or handicaps in performing self-care functions have been found to be quite useful, and a number of geriatric rating scales fall into this category. This type of assessment is reflected in the work of Kelman and Muller (Kelman, 1962; Kelman & Muller, 1962; Muller, 1961); Watson and Fulton (1967); and Katz and his associates (Katz, Ford, Moskowitz, Jackson, and Jaffe, 1963; Katz, Downs, Cash, and Grotz, 1970); and Gurel and Davis (1967). The Index of Independence in Activities of Daily Living (ADL) developed by Katz and his colleagues is probably the most widely used and empirically studied of these instruments.

The ADL index summarizes overall performance in six functions, namely, bathing, dressing, going to the toilet, transfering (movement in and out of bed and in and out of a chair), continence, and feeding (Katz et al., 1963). Index scores range from A, indicative of independent functioning in all six areas, to G, which represents dependence in all six types of activity. The instrument was developed as a tool for accumulating objective, quantitative data about prognosis and the dynamics of disability in the aging process. It has also been used for assessment of patient care needs, to evaluate the effectiveness of treatment, and as a teaching aid in rehabilitation. The ADL index has been found useful for these purposes in a wide variety of settings, including all types of residences, general hospitals, rehabilitation hospitals, extended care units, nursing homes, custodial care institutions, private medical practices, and housing projects for the aged. Thousands of evaluations have been made across this range of settings. A summary review of the clinical and research applications of this index of ADL is available in Katz et al. (1970).

Functional assessment scales that focus solely upon self-care activities have been criticized by Gurel, Linn and Linn (1972) as being too narrow, although these authors do not dispute the utility of such scales despite their limited focus. Gurel et al. argue for more comprehensive rating scales that take into account behaviors related to mental and psychological functioning as well as behaviors reflecting phsyical functioning. A number of more comprehensive scales of this sort have been developed. The most standard of these are the Stockton Geriatric Rating Scale (Meer and Baker, 1966), the Physical and Mental Impairment-Of-Function Evaluation (PAMIE) Scale (Gurel et al. 1972), and the Geriatric Rating Scale developed at

Bronx State Hospital (Plutchik, Conte, Liebeman, Baker, Grossman and Lehman, 1970). The range of domains of functioning tapped by such scales is quite broad, as is evidenced by the findings of Gurel et al. (1972), who report that factor analysis of their data (collected on 845 males being placed in veteran-nursing homes) yielded ten factors that the authors describe as self-care dependent, belligerent-irritable, mentally disorganized, anxious-depressed, bedfast-moribund, behaviorally deteriorated, paranoid-suspicious, sensorimotor impaired, withdrawn-apathetic, and ambulatory.

Plutchik et al. (1970) made dual ratings on 86 patients (a subgroup of the 207 patients, both male and female, in geriatric wards in Bronx State Hospital) and found that the correlation between the ratings made by the two judges were .87, indicating that a scale of this type can be highly reliable. The aforementioned authors also present data to argue for the validity of their scales. Plutchik et al. published normative data with their study that provide a frame of reference against which future patients may be evaluated for purposes of placement, selection, treatment, and research. It should be noted that the content of these scales, the nature of the research conducted on and/or with them, the characteristics of the populations on which research was conducted, etc., differ considerably. The clinician or researcher contemplating using this type of instrument would be well advised to consult the work of the authors cited above to determine which specific scale seems most suited to his particular needs.

Brief mention might also be made parenthetically of rating scales that attempt to tap more subjective factors. Bloom and Blenkner (1970) suggest that the psychologist who is developing and assessing service programs should be attentive to the "contentment" level of the patients he is serving. They are developing a contentment scale that yields a quantitative index. Cautious about recommending their scale for use at this point, they note that "although it has been used with three different populations of older persons (over 500 persons), further work on the Contentment Index is planned before it can be claimed to be a standardized research instrument usable for evaluating the effectiveness of other experimental programs and in studies of social epidemiology which are so vitally needed". Although other scales have been developed to assess life satisfaction (e.g., Adams, 1969), these have tended to grow out of theoretical research and would appear to have limited utility for the psychologist in his roles of clinician and program evaluator.

Although the "self-care" and "general physical psychosocial" rating scales discussed above appear to have been established as valuable fixtures in the psychologist's armamentarium, they are still relatively primitive. Powell Lawton (1970a) has observed that "a single assessment device is not likely to be able to discriminate behavior throughout the entire range of complexity." He describes a taxonomy of categories of target behavior of varying complexity that are potentially amendable to functional assessment, and proposes that "a full assessment should contain enough instruments to represent (a) all the important levels of behavior, (b) the major ranges of complexity within each level, and (c) the major range of normative competence . . . ." Lawton's stimulating thinking goes beyond the scope of the present discussions, but the interested reader is referred to Lawton's 1970 and 1972 publications.

A pertinent problem associated with use of the rating scales is whether to rate the patient according to his lowest, typical, or highest level of functioning. The authors who explicitly speak to this issue evidently favor rating "typical" functioning. For instance, Katz et al. (1970) indicate that patients being assessed on the index of ADL are rated "on actual performance and not on ability." This would appear to be a reasonable way of proceeding for the efficacy of research evaluating program as long as he is sensitive to and avoids environmental artifacts. Katz et al. have listed some common sources of artifactual interference with their ratings. "For safety reasons, some hospitals require nurses to supervise patients who shower or get into tubs. During the first few days in the hospital, patients are sometimes kept in bed until the staff can assess their behavior and the degree of dependence permissible. In some nursing homes, patients are kept in bed and not permitted to dress . . . for safety and convenience, water for bathing and clothes are sometimes brought to patients. All these special conditions can result in . . . ratings that are lower than they might be in the absence of such restrictions. A test of actual functional level is possible and is indicated for certain studies."

However, the clinician who is assessing the extent to which a given patient will require a supportive environment would gain valuable information by assessing level of functioning under the optional circumstances. Consider, for instance, a patient whose score on a rating scale suggests severe impairment, but whose behavior during the assessment procedures was regressed because of manageable motivational (e.g., depression) and/or environmental (e.g., lack of reinforcement and stimulation) factors. The clinician assessing such a patient must have a reasonable idea (ideally bolstered by objective data) of the extent to which the deficit he has found is attributable to reversible variables as opposed to "irreversible" deterioration. That is, it would seem advisable to reevaluate the patient after identifiable manageable factors have been therapeutically altered. If the clinician fails to do this, the patient may continue to function with an unde- tected "excess disability". Excess disability has been defined as "the discrepancy which exists when the person's functional incapacity is greater than warranted by the actual impairment" (Brody, Kleban, Lawton, and Silverman, 1971; Kahn, 1965) that will be exacerbated by transferring him to an environment where he will be allowed to become more dependent because of his assumed deficit in capacity. Pincus and Wood (1970) have noted that if "staff hold low expecta- tions of the residents' abilities . . . the residents in time begin to live up to their expectations." In short, a diagnostic formulation under optimal circumstances may have the effect of setting in motion or consolidating a self-fulfilling prophecy that is countertherapeutic.

The testing of limits of functioning through environmental manipulations is in itself a form of ecologically oriented assessment (and treatment). What is being proposed here is a behaviorial analysis of performance deficit to determine the extent to which the deficit is remedied with the introduction of appropriate motivating rein- forcers, or, in other words, to determine whether the deficit is one of performance (and therefore treatable) or capacity. Lindsley (1964) has recommended the use of experimental assessment of geriatric patients in free operant laboratories to assess behavioral deficits. Assuming that a deficit is found that appears to be one of capacity, the diagnostic role of an innovative clinician is not necessarily com- plete. He may pursue his assessment further to determine whether the patient is capable of compensating for his deficit when provided with a "prosthetic environment." For instance, social relationships of some elderly persons may break down because of feeble voices; such a problem (both the primary problem of feebleness of voice and the secondary problem of impaired social functioning) might be resolved by provision of a throat microphone and transistorized amplifiers (Lindsley, 1964). See this stimulating article on "geriatric behavioral prosthetics" for many more suggestions for reducing deficit through provision of a prosthetic environment.

A final form of ecological assessment is represented by the work of Pincus (Pincus, 1968; Pincus and Wood, 1970). Pincus has de- veloped an instrument he calls the "Home for the Aged Description Questionnaire" (HDQ) to assess institutional settings for the aged. The specific environmental factors that the instrument was designed to tap are *privacy:* "the degree to which the environment allows the resident to establish and maintain a personal domain which is not open to public view or use and into which the institution will not transgress"; *freedom:* "the degree to which the resident must adjust his life to imposed rules and discipline and the extent to which he is permitted, encouraged, or required to exercise any choice, decision-making, or initiative"; *resources*: "the degree to which the environment provides opportunities for the resident to engage in a variety of work and leisure activities and to participate in social interaction with staff and other residents in a variety of social roles and statuses other than the patient role. . ."; and *integration*: "the degree to which the environment affords opportunities for communication and interaction with the larger heterogenous community (people and places) in which the institution is located" (Pincus and Wood, 1970). Factor analysis of item ratings yielded a new factor in addition to the four described above. This fifth factor, *personalization*, pertains to the "social distance between the staff and residents (e.g., staff knowing the residents by name, having friendly chats with them, and taking a personal interest in them)"—(Pincus and Wood, 1970). Pincus and Wood caution that the research conducted with the scale is limited and less than adequate. The development of this sort of instrument, although presently in a rudimentary stage, may prove valuable to the clinician concerned with finding an environment suited to his aged client's needs as well as to the researcher.

SUMMARY

This chapter has dealt with the adaptability of our present diagnostic techniques in the evaluation of the aged person, and with some new trends such as the ecological assessment. This review of the present level of our psychodiagnostic techniques indicated that there is a definite lack of reliable norms for the older age groups. This being the case, the clinician confronted with the necessity of evaluating an older patient must make use of present diagnostic tools with the utmost care. He needs to consider the effects of psychological factors described by Oberleder (1964), who states that "the greatest difference in working with the older Subject is that physical, psychosocial and anxiety factors increase with age, tests become more threatening generally, and performance more likely to be affected by non-test factors, all of which must be considered in interpreting test results."

It is necessary to keep in mind that the older individual brings, in addition to the usual problems encountered by the young, problems unique to his group. The older patient may be confronted with the imminence of death; he may be depressed, or bordering on this condition. His memory in certain areas has begun to fail, his relationship with others has changed, and his own self-esteem has decreased. Practical issues such as poor health, finances, and housing also should be considered. All of these factors need to be considered and used in order to evaluate the older individual's test performance.

The new trend exemplified by the ecological assessment techniques directs itself to the task of determining what an older person can do given a particular situation or a choice of situations. This approach lends itself very well to the task of finding dimensions of functioning and tasks with which to measure them, which may be important in the rehabilitation therapy or the screening and placement of the older individual.

The ecological assessment techniques may provide a technology both of choosing relevant areas to test, and of helping the older person, or those who can help him, to plan and function in an environment that is congruent with his capacities.

Despite the fact that our current psychodiagnostic techniques seem to be lacking in adequate norms for the older population, it is hoped that the comments in this chapter will lead us to think with Oberleder (1967) that the typical diagnostic test battery in use today may be adaptable for use with the aging, provided we keep in mind the limitations and the needs of the older individual.

REFERENCES

Aaronson, B.S. Age and sex influences on MMPI profile peak distribution in an abnormal population. *Journal of Consulting Psychology*, 1958, *22*: 203-06.

———. A dimension of personality change with aging. *Journal of Clinical Psychology*, 1960, *16*: 63-65.

Adams, D.L. Analysis of life satisfaction index. *Journal of Gerontology*, 1969, *24*: 470-74.

Ames, L.B. Age changes in the Rorschach responses of a group of older individuals. *Journal of Genetic Psychology*, 1960, *97*: 257-85.

Ames, L.B.; Learned, J.; Metraux, R.W.; and Walker, R.N. *Rorschach responses in old age*. New York: Harper Bros., 1954.

Ammons, R.B. and Ammons, C.H. The Quick Test: provisional manual. *Psychological Reports*, 1962, *11*: 11-161.

Bayley, N. and Oden, M. The maintenance of intellectual ability in gifted adults. *Journal of Gerontology*, 1955, *10*: 91-107.

Benton, A.L. *The revised visual retention test. Clinical and experimental application*. New York: The Psychological Corporation, 1963.

Berger, L.; Bernstein, A.; Klein, E.; Cohen, J.; and Lucas, G. Effects of aging and pathology on the factorial structure of intelligence. *Journal of Consulting Psychology*, 1964, *28*: 199-207.

Birren, J.E. A factorial analysis of the Wechsler-Bellevue Scale given to an elderly population. *Journal of Consulting Psychology*, 1952, *16*: 399-405.

Bloom, M. and Blenkner, M. Assessing functioning of older persons living in the community. *The Gerontologist*, 1970, *10*: 31-37.

Bolton, N.; Britton, P.G.; and Savage, R.D. Some normative data on the WAIS and its indices in an aged population. *Journal of Clinical Psychology,* 1966, *22*: 184-88.

Bolton, N.; Savage, R.D.; and Roth, M. The modified word learning test and the aged psychiatric patient. *British Journal of Psychiatry,* 1967, *113*, 1139-40.

Botwinick, J. *Cognitive processes in maturity and old age.* New York: Springer, 1967.

Brody, E.M., Kleban, M.H.; Lawton, M.P.; and Silverman, H.A. Excess disabilities of mentally impaired aged: Impact of individualized treatment. *The Gerontologist,* 1971, *11*: 124-33.

Britton, P.G. and Savage, R.D. The MMPI and the aged: Some normative data from a community sample. *British Journal of Psychiatry,* 1965, *112*: 941-943.

Brozek, Joseph. Personality changes with age: an item analysis of the MMPI. *Journal of Gerontology,* 1955, *10*: 194-206.

Buros, O.K., ed. *The seventh mental measurements yearbook.* Highland Park, New Jersey: The Gryphon Press, 1972.

Calden, G. and Hokanson, J.E. The influence of age on MMPI responses. *Journal of Clinical Psychology,* 1959, *15*: 194-95.

Canter, A.A. A background interference procedure to increase sensitivity of the Bender-Gestalt Test to organic brain disorder. *Journal of Consulting Psychology,* 1966, *30*: 91-97.

Chesrow, E.J.; Wasika, P.H.; and Reinitz, A.H. A psychometric evaluation of aged white males. *Geriatrics,* 1949, *4*: 169-77.

Cohen, J. The factorial structure of the WAIS between early and old age. *Journal of Consulting Psychology,* 1957, *21*: 283-90.

Cosin, L.Z.; Mort, M.; Post, F.; Westropp, C.; and Williams, M. 50 cases of persistent senile confusion. *International Journal of Social Psychiatry,* 1957, *3:* 195-202.

Davidson, H.H. and Druglov, L. Personality characteristics of the institutionalized aged. *Journal of Consulting Psychology,* 1952, *16*: 5-12.

Davies, A. The influence of age on Trail Making Test performance. *Journal of Clinical Psychology,* 1968, *24*: 96-98.

Doppelt, J.E. and Wallace W.L. Standardization of the Wechsler Adult Intelligence Scale for older persons. *Journal of Abnormal and Social Psychology,* 1955, *51*: 371-81.

Doust, J.W.; Schneider, R.A.; Talland, G.A.; Walsh, M.A.; and Braker, G.B. Studies on the physiology of awareness: the correlation between intelligence and anoxemia. *Journal of Nervous and Mental Disorders,* 1953, *117* (5): 383-98.

Eisdorfer, C. Rorschach performance and intellectual functioning in the aged. *Journal of Gerontology,* 1963, *18* (4): 358-63.

———. The WAIS performance of the aged: a retest evaluation. *Journal of Gerontology,* 1967, *18*: 169-72.

Eisdorfer, C.; Busse, E.W.; and Cohen, L.D. The WAIS performance of an aged sample: the relationship between verbal and performance I.Q.'s. *Journal of Gerontology,* 1959, *14* (2): 197-201.

Eisdorfer, C. and Cohen, L.I. The generality of the WAIS standardization for the aged: a regional comparison. *Journal of Abnormal and Social Psychology*, 1961, *62* (3): 520–27.

Faschingbauer, T.R. A 166-item written short form of the group MMPI: the FAM. *Journal of Consulting and Clinical Psychology*, 1974, *42*, 645–55.

Field, G. Two types of tables for use with Wechsler's intelligence scales. *Journal of Clinical Psychology*, 1960, *16*: 3–7.

Fink, M.; Green, T.; and Bender, M. The Face-Hand Test as a dianostic sign of organic mental syndrome. *Neurology*, 1952, *2*: 46–58.

Geerstman, R.H. Factor analysis of Rorschach scoring categories for a population of normal subjects. *Journal of Consulting Psychology*, 1962, *26*: 20–25.

Gendreau, L.; Roach, T.; and Gendreau, P. Assessing the intelligence of the aged person: report on the Quick Test. *Psychological Reports*, 1973, *32* (2): 475–80.

Granick, S. and Friedman, A.S. The effects of education on the decline of psychometric test performance with age. *Journal of Gerontology*, 1967, *22*: 191–95.

Grossman, C.; Worshawsky, F.; and Hertz, M. Rorschach studies on personality characteristics of a group of institutionalized old people. (Abstract). *Journal of Gerontology*, 1951, *6* (suppl, to no. 3): 97.

Gurel, L. and Davis, J.E., Jr. A survey of self-care dependency in psychiatric patients. *Hospital and Community Psychiatry*, 1967, *18*: 135–38.

Gurel, L.; Linn, M.W.; and Linn, B.S. Physical and mental impairment of function evaluation in the aged: The PAMIE Scale. *Journal of Gerontology*, 1972, *27*: 83–90.

Gynther, M.D. and Shimkunas, A. Age and MMPI performance. *Journal of Consulting Psychology*, 1966, *30* (2): 118–21.

Hain, J.D. The Bender-Gestalt Test: A scoring method for identifying brain damage. *Journal of Consulting Psychology*, 1964, *28*: 34–40.

Hardyck, C.B. Sex differences in personality changes with age. *Journal of Gerontology*, 1964, *19*: 78–82.

Hathaway, S.R. and McKinley, J.C. *The minnesota multiphasic personality inventory manual revised.* New York: The Psychological Corp., 1951.

Hooper, H.E. A study in the construction and preliminary standardization of a visual organization test for the use in the measurement of organic deterioration. Master's Thesis, University of Southern California, 1948.

———. Use of the Hooper Visual Organization Test in the differentiation of organic brain pathology from normal, psychoneurotic and schizophrenic reaction. Paper read at meetings of the American Psychological Association, Washington, D.C., September 1952. (Abstract.) *Amer. Psychol.*, 1952, 7: 350.

———. *The hooper visual organization test manual.* Los Angeles: Western Psychological Services, 1958.

Hopkins, B. and Roth, M. Psychological test performance in patients over sixty, II. Paraphrenia, arteriosclerotic psychosis and acute confusion. *Journal of Mental Science*, 1953, *99*: 451–63.

Inglis, J. A paired associate learning test for use with elderly psychiatric patients. *Journal of Mental Science*, 1959, *105*: 440–43.

Irving, G.; Robinson, R.A.; and McAdam, W. The validity of some cognitive tests in the diagnosis of dementia. *British Journal of Psychiatry*, 1970, *117*: 149-56.

Jarvick, L.F. and Falek, A. Intellectual stability and survival in the aged. *Journal of Gerontology*, 1963, *17*: 173-76.

Jarvick, L.F.; Kallman, F.J.; and Falek, A. Intellectual changes in aged twins. *Journal of Gerontology*, 1962, *17*: 289-94.

Jones, H.E. and Conrad, H.S. The growth and decline of intelligence: a study of a homogeneous population between the ages of ten and sixty. *Genetic Psychology Monographs*, 1933, *13*: 233-98.

Kahn, R.L.; Goldfarb, A.T.; Pollack, M.; and Peck, A. Brief objective measures for the determination of mental status in the aged. *American Journal of Psychiatry*, 1960, *117*: 326-28.

Kahn, R.S. Comments. In Proceedings of the New York House Institute on the Mentally Impaired Aged. Philadelphia: Philadelphia Geriatric Center, 1965.

Katz, S.; Downs, T.D.; Cash, H.R.; and Gratz, R.C. Progress in the development of the index of ADL. *The Gerontologist*, 1970, *10*: 20-30.

Katz, S.; Ford, A.B.; Moskowitz, R.W.; Jackson, B.A.; and Jaffe, M.W. Studies of illness in the aged. The index of ADL, a standardized measure of biological and psychosocial function. *Journal of the American Medical Association*, 1963, *185*: 914-19.

Kelman, H.R. An experiment in the rehabilitation of nursing home patients. *Public Health Reports*, 1962, 77: 356-66.

Kelman, H.R. and Muller, J.N. Rehabilitation of nursing home residents. *Geriatrics*, 1962, *17*: 402-11.

Kerejarto, M. von. Zur altersstabulitat des Benton Tests. Unpublished paper, 1963.

Kincannon, J. Prediction of the standard MMPI scale scores from 71 items: the mini-mult. *Journal of Consulting and Clinical Psychology*, 1968, *32*, 319-25.

Kleemeier, R.W. Intellectual change in the senium. *Proceedings of the Social Statistics Section of the American Statistical Association*, Washington, D.C. pp. 290-95. 1962.

————. Intellectual change in the senium or death and the I.Q. Presidential Address, Division of Maturity and Old Age, American Psychological Association, 1961.

Klopfer, W.G. Personality patterns of old age. *Rorschach Research Exchange*, 1946, *10*: 145-66.

Kornetsky, C.H. Minnesota Multiphasis Personality Inventory results obtained from a population of aged men. In Birren et al., eds., *Human aging*, pp. 253-56. Bethesda, Md.: U.S. Department of Health, Education and Welfare, NIMH, 1963.

Kuhlen, R.G. and Kerl, C. The Rorschach performance of 100 elderly males. (Abstract.) *Journal of Gerontology*, 1951, *6* (supp. to no. 3): 115.

Lawton, M.P. Assessment, integration and environments for older people. *The Gerontologist*, 1970a, *10*: 38-46.

————. Gerontology in clinical psychology, and vice-versa. *Aging and Human Development*, 1970b, *1*: 147-59.

————. Assessing the competence of older people. In D. Kent, R. Kastenbaum, and S. Sherwood, eds., *Research planning and action for the elderly*, p. 122-43. New York: Behavioral Publications, 1972.

Levine, N.R. Validation of the Quick Test for intelligence screening of the elderly. *Psychological Reports*, 1971, *29* (1): 167-72.

Light, B.A. and Amick, J.H. Rorschach responses of Normal Aged. *Journal of Projective Techniques*, 1956, *20*: 185-95.

Lindsley, O.R. Geriatric behavioral prosthetics. In R. Kastembaum, ed., *New thoughts on old age*, pp. 41-60. New York: Springer, 1964.

Loranger, A.W. and Misiak, H.K. The performance of aged females on fine-non-language tests of intellectual functions. *Journal of Clinical Psychology*, 1960, *16* (2): 189-91.

Markson, E.W. and Levitz, G. A Guttman Scale to assess memory loss among the elderly. *The Gerontologist*, 1973, *13*: 337-40.

Mason, C.F. and Ganzler, H. Adult Norms for the Shipley Institute of Living Scale and Hooper Visual Organization Test, based on age and education. *Journal of Gerontology*, 1964, *19*: 419-24.

Meer, B. and Baker, J.A. The Stockton Geriatric Rating Scale. *Journal of Gerontology*, 1966, *21*: 392-403.

Miles, C.C. and Miles, W.R. The correlation of intelligence scores and chronological age from early to later maturity. *American Journal of Psychology*, 1932, *44*: 44-78.

Muller, J.N. Rehabilitation evaluation: Some social and clinical problems. *American Journal of Public Health*, 1961, *51*: 403-10.

Neugarten, B.L.; Havinghurst, R.J.; and Tolun, S.S. The measurement of life satisfaction. *Journal of Gerontology*, 1961, *16*: 134-43.

Newcombe, F. and Steinberg, B. Some aspects of learning and memory function in older psychiatric patients. *Journal of Gerontology*, 1964, *19*: 490-93.

Oberleder, M. Effects of psycho-social factors on test results of the aging. *Psychological Reports*, 1964, *14*: 383-87.

————. Adapting current psychological techniques for use in testing the aged. *The Gerontologist*, 1967, 7: 3.

Owens, W.A., Jr. Age and mental abilities: a longitudinal study. *Genetic Psychology Monographs*, 1953, *48*: 3-54.

Pincus, A. The definition and measurement of the institutional environmental in homes for the aged. *The Gerontologist*, 1968, *8*: 207-210.

Pincus, A. and Wood, V. Methodological issues in measuring the environment in institutions for the aged and its impact on residents. *Aging and Human Development*, 1970, *1*: 117-26.

Plutchik, R.; Conte, H.; and Lieberman, M. Development of a scale (GIES) for assessment of cognitive and perceptual functioning in geriatric patients. *Journal of the American Geriatrics Society*, 1971, *19* (4): 614-23.

Plutchik, R.; Conte, H.; Lieberman, M.; Baker, M.; Grossman, J.; and Lehrman, N. Reliability and validity of a scale for assessing the functioning of geriatric patients. *Journal of the American Geriatrics Society*, 1970, *18*: 491-500.

Postema, G. and Schell, R.E. Some MMPI evidence of seemingly greater neurotic behavior among older people. *Journal of Clinical Psychology*, 1967, *23*: 140-43.

Prados, M. and Fried, E.G. Personality structure in the older age groups. *Journal of Clinical Psychology*, 1947, *17*: 302-304.

Raven, J.C. *Guide to using the coloured progressive matrices*. London, Great Britain: Lewis and Co., 1965.

Reed, H.B.C. and Reitan, R.M. Changes in psychological test performance associated with the normal aging process. *Journal of Gerontology*, 1963, *18*: 271-74.

Reitan, R.M. The distribution according to age of a psychologic measure dependent upon organic brain functions. *Journal of Gerontology*, 1955a, *10* (3): 338-40.

———. The relations of the Trail Making Test to organic brain damage. *Journal of Consulting Psychology*, 1955b, *19*: 393-95.

———. The comparative effects of brain damage on the halstead impairment index and the wechsler bellevue scale. *Journal of Clinical Psychology*, 1959, *15*, 281-85.

———. Psychological deficit. *Annual Review of Psychology*, 1962, *13*, 415-44.

Riddell, S.A. The relationship between tests of organic involvement, memory impairment and diagnosis in elderly psychiatric patients. *British Journal of Social and Clinical Psychology*, 1962, *1*: 31-37.

Riegel, K.M. and Riegel, K.F. A comparison and re-interpretation of factor structures of the W-B, the WAIS and the HAWIE on aged persons. *Journal of Consulting Psychology*, 1962, *26*: 31-37.

Riegel, K.F.; Riegel, R.M.; and Meyer, G. A study of dropout rates in longitudinal research in aging and the prediction of death. *Journal of Personality and Social Psychology*, 1967, *4*: 342-48.

Rorschach, H. *Psychodiagnostics*. New York: Grune and Stratton, 1942.

Roth, M. and Hopkins, E. Psychological test performance in patients over sixty. I. Senile psychosis and the affective disorders of old age. *Journal of Mental Science*, 1953, *99*: 439-50.

Savage, R.D. Psychometric assessment and clinical diagnosis in the aged. In D.W. Kay and A. Wolk, eds., *Recent development in psychogeriatrics. British Journal of Psychiatry Special Publication, No. 6*, 1971.

Savage, R.D.; Britton, P.G.; George, S.; O'Connor, D.; and Hall, E.H. A developmental investigation of intellectual functioning on the community aged. *Journal of Genetic Psychology*, 1972, *121* (1): 163-67.

Schaie, K.W. and Strother, C.R. A cross-sequential study of age changes in cognitive behavior. *Psychological Bulletin*, 1968(a) *70*: 671-80.

———. The effect of time and cohort differences on the interpretation of age changes in cognitive behavior. *Multivariate Behavioral Research*, 1968(b), *3*: 259-94.

Swensen, W.M. Structured personality testing in the aged, an MMPI study of the geriatric populations. *Journal of Clinical Psychology,* 1961, *17*: 302–304.

Thaler, M.B. The application of three theories of personality to the Rorschach of seventy-five aged subjects. Doctoral dissertation, University of Denver, 1952.

Watson, C.G. and Fulton, J.R. Treatment potential of the psychiatric-medically infirm. I. Self-care, independence. *Journal of Gerontology,* 1967, *22*: 449–55.

Wechsler, D. *Manual for the Wechsler Adult Intelligence Scale.* New York: Psychological Corporation, 1955.

————. *The measurement and appraisal of adult intelligence.* 4th ed. Baltimore: Williams and Wilkins, 1958.

Wechsler, David. *A standard memory scale for clinical use.* Provincetown, Mass.: The Journal Press, 1945.

Williams, M. The effect of past experience on mental test preformance in the elderly. *British Journal of Medical Psychology,* 1960, *33*: 215–19.

————. Geriatric patients. In P. Mittler, ed., *The psychological assessment of mental and mental handicaps.* London: Methuen and Co. Ltd., 1970.

Wolk, R.L. and Wolk, R.B. *Manual of the gerontological apperception test.* New York: Behavioral Publications, 1972.

Chapter 5

A Psychological Theory of the Later Years: C.G. Jung

W. Derek Shows
Duke University Medical Center

A recent survey of the American research literature on aging and human development revealed a total lack of any attempt to apply the theoretical frame of reference of Carl G. Jung to the study of middle and late life. Frequent reference is made in the literature to the fact that there are ample psychological theories of child development and to the inadequacies of the extension of such theories to the continuing development and changes that occur during adulthood (Neugarten et al., 1964). The most frequently occurring theoretical frame of reference in the literature on aging in terms of personality theories appears to be Freudian psychoanalytic theory and its later extensions are exemplified by Erikson and the ego-psychologists, e.g., Hartmann. In general, psychoanalytic theory tends to focus on the psychosexual development of an individual during the first five or six years of life, and the gradual unfolding and further development of the influence of these childhood factors into and throughout adult life. The need for a specific psychological theory of adult development, particularly during the middle and late years, has also frequently been cited in the aging literature (Neugarten, 1968).

In view of this state of affairs, it is rather surprising that the psychological theory of C.G. Jung and its practical and research implications have been overlooked entirely. Jung has maintained explicitly that Freudian psychoanalytic theory is most applicable to the *first half of life* in which the major developmental tasks involve learning to deal with one's instinctual drives, establishing one's identity and independence, developing interpersonal intimacy in the form of marriage and formation of a family life, and developing and utilizing optimally one's abilities in work and society. On the other hand, Jung emphasized that his psychological theory applies primarily to the *second half of life* in which the developmental tasks involve a reassessing of one's life and goals, an increasing awareness of and emphasis upon one's inner life, an attempt to put one's life in perspective, and preparation for death. Freudian psychoanalytic theory has sometimes been called a *preparation for living*, in contrast to Jungian theory as a *preparation for dying.* The intent here is not to pit one theory against the other, which is most frequently done when these two theories are compared and contrasted in a single discussion, but rather to suggest that the two theories are not necessarily mutually exclusive and may indeed be complementary.

Given the apparent fact that there is not a widespread familiarity with Jungian theory in American psychology, it would seem necessary to begin with a brief presentation of some of the basic tenets of Jungian theory before attempting to indicate its relevance to a theory of aging or, at least, a developmental theory of the middle and late years. Jung's theory deals with the psychological development of the individual personality. While Jung did not pay a great deal of attention to the first half of life, he did begin with the basic point of view that the human psyche is, at the onset, essentially undifferentiated, and that personality development is then a progressive course of differentiation and integration of the functions of the psyche. Jung postulated four basic psychic functions that are constitutionally present in every individual: thinking, intuition, feeling, and sensation. A psychic function involves primarily a mode of apprehending and assimilating psychic data, regardless of their content and source. These functions represent four basic ways of dealing with incoming data, i.e., with events occurring in either the external or internal world. These functions describe what a person does with these data and events. They describe ways of adapting to external and internal life events. Briefly, *thinking* is the function that seeks to apprehend the world and adjust to it by means of thought or cognition, i.e., logical inferences. The function of *feeling*, on the other hand, apprehends the world through an evaluation based on the pleasant or unpleasant feelings, acceptance or rejection. Both of these functions are termed rational, because both constitute evaluations and judgements; thinking evaluates through cognition from the standpoint of "true-false;" feeling through the emotions from the standpoint of "pleasant-unpleasant." As determinants of behavior, these two basic functions are mutually exclusive at any given time; either one or the other predominates. Jung called the other two functions, sensation and intuition, the irrational functions because they operate not through judgement but with mere perceptions that are not evaluated or interpreted. *Sensation* is said to be the perception of things as they are, concretely. *Intuition* is also said to be perception, but less through the conscious apparatus of the senses than through the capacity for an unconscious "inner perception" of the inherent potentiality of things. These two functions are likewise antithetical and mutually exclusive (Jacobi, 1962).

Although everyone constitutionally possesses all four functions, the individual develops only one of these as the dominant mode of adaptation that gives the conscious attitude its direction and quality. In addition, an individual usually develops and uses to a lesser degree a second or auxiliary function, which gives a particular flavor to the superior function. That is, the auxiliary function adds its own particular influence to the primary mode of experiencing and interacting with the world. For example, a person who has differentiated and developed primarily the thinking function and secondarily has developed the intuitive function may show a distinct preference for involvement with theoretical ideas in a profession such as physics rather than a preference for the kind of intricate, detailed reasoning required of an engineer, which would be more character-istic of a thinking type individual whose auxiliary function is sensation.

To complicate matters further, Jung also distinguished two basic attitudes of *introversion* and *extraversion*, which determine an individual's response to objects in the outer and inner world, the nature of one's subjective experience, and even the compensatory action of one's unconscious. The introverted person's inner sub-jective experience is the primary determinant of his behavior, his orientation in the world, and his locus of control. The extraverted person, on the other hand, orients himself primarily in terms of external relationships and events. Thus, his behavior is more determined by and his attention more directed toward the object of the task engaged in, the norms of the particular group or culture with whom he is interacting, the demands of the situation, and so forth. The four basic functions and the two basic attitudes in interaction with each other form the basis for a rather sophisticated typology of personality (Jung, 1971).

The most essential developmental task of the first half of life then is to differentiate and establish the constitutional function that will best enable one to gain a foothold in the world and to meet the demands of his early environment. The overdifferentiation of the superior function, which is almost inevitable with the passing of years in the course of normal development, results nearly always in an imbalance in the psychic system and in tensions that represent the main problems of the second half of life. In the middle years, the neglected functions and unconscious attitude begin to claim their rights for differentiation and development. For the goal is always psychic totality, the ideal solution in which at least three of the four functions and both types of attitudes are made as conscious and operational as possible (Jacobi, 1962). Thus, in the second half of life, personality changes begin to occur in which the individual begins to take into account the undeveloped aspects of his personality.

When there is imbalance in the psychic system due to over-development of the superior function and neglect of the remaining functions, the individual becomes aware of experiencing a vague sense of dissatisfaction, self-alienation, and gnawing doubts about his life and accomplishments thus far. This is what has often been referred to as the middle-aged crisis. Such a crisis occurs in a person who has focused most of his efforts in developing and establishing himself in a particular line of work and in a particular style of life. It may happen that when he has achieved his life goal(s), he discovers that his achievement does not bring him the satisfaction and happiness that he expected and his considerable accomplishments may seem meaningless and worthless to him at this point. Then the process of reviewing his life, and his success to date, begins and he asks himself what are often difficult, disturbing questions. When this kind of crisis occurs, the individual may initiate changes in his life, e.g., change jobs or seek a new profession. The usual example given of the person experiencing this type of middle-aged crisis is either the hard-driving business executive or the bored housewife. Another example might be found among the astronauts, who were for awhile the heroes of our American society, representing the epitome of scientific development and achievement—the super scientist. It has been interesting to note that several of these individuals, after reaching the peak of their careers in the aerospace industry, have gone into apparently entirely different ventures, such as ecology projects, parapsychology, evangelism, and politics. These can be seen as individuals who developed exclusively one function of their personality in the first half of life and then in the middle years the other parts of their personality take over and manifest themselves by rather dramatic changes in behavior. Jungian psychology, thus, may offer a frame of reference within which to systematically study the changes that begin to occur in the middle or late years.

Sarason, Sarason, and Cowden (1975) most recently indicated the increasing numbers of educated, professional people who "seek a career change, be that within or between fields of work" and describe a large and growing group of middle-aged individuals who experience feelings of boredom, of being locked into a pattern of work behavior that has become uninteresting and void of challenge, imprisoned and unfulfilled. They describe "many of the aged (or not so aged)" who look back on their lives and ask the disturbing question, "Was it worth it?" Much of their discussion seems relevant both to the field of psychology of aging and the Jungian personality theory described above.

The conclusions reached by researchers in the field of aging and human development are strikingly congruent with some of the conceptual notions of Jungian theory. From research studies reported by Neugarten (1964), the conclusion was made that different modes of dealing with impulse life seem to become salient with increasing age. She noted that preoccupation with the inner life becomes greater; emotional cathexes toward persons and objects in the external world seem to decrease; readiness to attribute activity and affect to persons in the environment is reduced; and there is a movement away from outer world toward inner world orientations. In discussing the contributions of these research studies to the theory of disengagement (as set forth by Cummings and Henry [1961]) in which aging is perceived as an inevitable and mutual withdrawal resulting in decreased interaction between the aging person and others in the social system(s) to which he belongs, Neugarten points out that the basic components of disengagement are in part intrinsic and in part responsive. She maintains that although personality processes should be seen as transactional throughout life and the personality as developing only through interactions between the individual and his environment, nevertheless, the increase in interiority has the characteristics of developmental change in much the same sense as do changes in earlier periods of life—that, as a result of the life history, with its accumulating record of adaptations to both biological and social events, there is a continually changing basis within the individual for perceiving and responding to new events in the outer world. In this sense, the basis of the age-related differences that emerged in these studies were attributed to the personality rather than to the social environment. The psychological components of disengagement seemed to precede the social components, since the increased inward orientation was measurable by the midforties in Neugarten's sample of well-functioning adults, well before the social losses of aging had occurred and well before the decrease in social interaction described by Cumming and Henry (1961) or the incompetency of performance in adult social roles described by

Havighurst (1957). These findings were furthermore interpreted as arguing against the implication that increased interiority and eccentricity of behavior in the aged follow a thinning of social interaction and a lessening of normative controls. Although there is undoubtedly an interaction effect existing between psychological and social forces of disengagement, the implication of these findings is that the psychological changes accompanying aging occur first before measurable changes in the extent of social interaction are in evidence.

Elsewhere, Neugarten (1968) has reported that in the middle years both sexes, but particularly men, talked of the new difference in the way time is perceived. Life becomes restructured in terms of *time left to live* rather than *time since birth*. In addition to this obvious reversal in the directionality of time perception, a particularly conspicuous feature of middle age is the awareness that time is finite. In short, Neugarten indicates that the middle years represent an important turning point in life with the restructuring of time and the formulation of new perceptions about self, time, and death. Introspection appears to increase noticeably, and contemplation, reflection, and self-evaluation become characteristic forms of mental life as one enters this critical period of development.

Novelists have long been aware of the important changes—reassessment of one's achievements and life goals, increase in inward living and self-awareness, and changes in values—that occur in the second half of life as exemplified in such works as Goethe's *Faust*, Hesse's *Steppenwolf*, Frisch's *I Am Not Stiller*, and Kazin's *The Arrangement*.

In her exposition of the psychology of C.G. Jung, Jacobi (1962) stated that in its broad outlines the individuation process is inherent in man, follows regular patterns, and falls into two main independent parts, characterized by contrasting and complementary qualities. These parts are the first and second halves of life. The task of the first half is considered to be "initiation into outward reality". The individual must fight his way from infancy to a differentiation and definition of his ego. He must establish himself firmly in real life, and confront and master the problems life raises: sexuality, entry into a profession, marriage, children, human relationships of all kinds. It is through the consolidation of the ego, the greatest possible differentiation of his constitutionally superior function and of the dominant attitude type, and the development of an appropriate persona that the individual acquires the tools needed for the work of adaptation to the demands of his environment. Only after this developmental task of the first half of life has been completed does the developmental task of the second half, "the initiation into the inner reality," become a concomitant necessity. The individual can now turn his energies toward those aspects of his personality that have thus far remained unconscious, undifferentiated, and undeveloped— the neglected intrapsychic realities. Thus, to build the wholeness of the personality is the task of middle life and also the preparation for death in the deepest sense of the word. For in this process of life, death is considered no less important than birth and, like birth, is viewed as an inseparable part of life. Theoretically, the older the individual becomes, the more veiled the outside world becomes, steadily losing in color, tone, and passion, and the more urgent become the demands of the inner world.

Finally, it should be noted that Maddox (1964) reviewed the evidence against disengagement theory as a general explanation of the aging process and stated in another article (1968) that, in the analysis of behavioral or attitudinal phenomena among the elderly, change rather than persistence is more often the focus. The use of cross-sectional, in contrast to longitudinal, design was criticized as resulting in attention being given neither to distinguishing changers from nonchangers nor to establishing baselines against which individual change many be measured in a meaningful way. Consequently, Maddox pointed out that both theoretical and methodological considerations suggest the relevance of studying persistence as well as change in the patterns of behavior and attitudes among elderly and aging persons seen longitudinally.

Thus, the status of disengagement theory as a general explanation of the aging process remains unsettled. However, one of the implications of Jungian personality theory is that changes occurring as part of the aging process may not all be in the same direction. If we take into account the individual personality types in the Jungian typology system, changes beginning to take place in the middle years would be in different directions and of different magnitudes, depending upon the developments during the first half of life. For example, Jungian theory postulates that persons extraverted initially will become somewhat more introverted during the later years, while the opposite will happen for persons initially introverted. The particular manifestations of these changes will vary as a function of the particular dominant function of the personality. Thus, in a cross-sectional sample people may be changing in different directions with differential manifestations of behavior, which would confound —and perhaps cancel out—statistical results if not accounted for. The application of Jungian theory of personality development to the study of personality change as a function of age could help clarify the confusing and often contradictory evidence relating to disengagement theory. Jungian psychology would also seem to offer considerable promise for major contributions toward a psychological theory of adulthood beyond the midpoint of life.

REFERENCES

Cumming, E. and Henry, W.E. *Growing old.* New York: Basic Books, 1961.

Havighurst, R.J. The social competence of middle-aged people. *Genetic Psychology Monographs*, 1957, *56:* 297–375.

Jacobi, J. *The psychology of C.G. Jung.* New Haven: Yale University Press, 1962.

Jung, C.G. *Psychological types.* Princeton: Princeton University Press, 1971.

Maddox, F.L. Disengagement theory: A critical evaluation. *The Gerontologist*, 1964, *14:* 80–83.

Maddox, G.L. Persistence of life style among the elderly: A longitudinal study of patterns of social activity in relation to life satisfaction. In B.L. Neugarten, ed., *Middle age and aging: A reader in social psychology.* Chicago: University of Chicago Press, 1968.

Neugarten, B.L. *Middle age and aging: A reader in social psychology.* Chicago: University of Chicago Press, 1968.

Neugarten, B.L. et al. *Personality in middle and late life.* New York: Atherton, 1964.

Sarason, S.B.; Sarason, E.K.; and Cowden, P. Aging and the nature of work. *American Psychologist*, 1975, *30:* 584–92.

 *Chapter 6*

Life Span Developmental Psychology and Clinical Geropsychology

Ilene C. Siegler
Duke University

I think that perhaps—and I do not say this critically—prosperity makes us resent and fear death and the humiliation of aging more than ever before, and we rightly fear aging rather than death. How many of us can really face the emotional and personal implications of·a visit to an old folk's home? It shows us throughout human history we have been putting up with the intolerable. These women were once beautiful, or at least young; these men were once people. It must be Faustian for prosperous nations to think this way as Yeats did about

> The death
> Of every beautiful eye
> Which made a catch in the breath.

We have put up with the idea of aging as a fact of life, but only so long as we saw no chance of doing anything about it. The time for that is over. If we see the possibility, we can change it, or at least try. (Comfort, 1970)

This chapter presents a review of literature in gerontology and developmental psychology from a life span perspective. It is aimed at providing baseline data on normal development as background information for clinical psychologists to use in their development of a clinical psychology of aging—geropsychology.

The needs for mental health services to the aged are already substantial and the evidence indicates the substantial needs will be increasing in the future. Birren and Woodruff (1973) estimated that, assuming a 2 percent need for psychiatric care in the population, 8,624 clinical psychologists would be needed to provide an average of three hours service for patient per year. Assuming 10 percent of the population in need at six hours per year, an estimated 86,235 clinicians will thus be needed. It is estimated that one-half of the general population in need will be middle-aged or older. The most staggering fact about their projections is that they were made for 1975.

Gurland (1973) in a chapter on the clinical psychology of aging written for the APA Task Force on Aging stated that: "Some illustrative examples of the characteristics that increase with age are: (a) cognitive impairment (b) some forms of depression (c) social isolation (d) admission to institutions and (e) diminished energy. A question is raised about which of such characteristics are part of normal aging and which should be attributed to pathology". Gurland could have also asked the question: Are these imputed characteristics true? And if so, at what age do they become operative and under what conditions? Lawton (1973) stated, at the present time, that there is no clinical psychology of aging. However, within the fields of developmental psychology and gerontology there has been concern, interest, and a significant amount of research over the past 30 to 40 years that should be relevant for the clinician.

As both gerontology and developmental psychology are inherently multidisciplinary fields, the material is organized into the following broad topic areas, which cut across many disciplinary boundaries: (1) methodology of life span developmental psychology; (2) biomedical data and brain behavior relationships: (3) experimental-developmental psychology; (4) personality, motivation, and adjustment; and (5) socialization, attitudes, and social roles.

METHODOLOGICAL ISSUES IN LIFE SPAN DEVELOPMENTAL PSYCHOLOGY

The goal of life span developmental psychology may be defined as an attempt to understand human development from conception till death, or, more simply, an attempt to understand the processes that define normal aging. Figure 6-1 is a schematic diagram of the population available for developmental studies between 1900 and the year 2000. Schaie (1965) first formalized this structure and suggested that any response or behavior is a function of chronological age, birth cohort, and the actual historical time when the measurements are made.

The main point of considering development this way is in understanding that when people differ in age, they also differ in life experiences. For example, the column labeled 1975 represents a five generation family. Differences between family members might be explained by (1) their maturational level or their age; (2) the fact that in 1975 it means something different to be 75 than to be 25 because the world treats you differently (index of current impact of culture—time of measurement); and (3) it makes a difference which cohort you were born into (the potential effect of spending childhood in the roaring twenties as opposed to the silent fifties.

While Schaie's developmental model has been most fruitful in generating important research and theoretical contributions to our understanding of the developmental processes, it could also serve as an important heuristic tool for the clinical practitioner in attempting to understand family dynamics, intergenerational conflict, and the relationship between the often "younger" therapist and the "older" client.

Of the seven descriptive terms used to describe the life span in Figure 6-1, four describe the first 25-50 years of life, two are used interchangeably for the next 35 years, and one term suffices for the last 35 years.

Parent-child, sibling, and peer relationships are seen as critical behavioral determinants earlier in the life span. Yet, as long as one's parents are alive—a parent-child relationship exists. When the "child" is 65 and the parent 87 the relationship may still be a significant one. A life span perspective is helpful in forcing consideration of both the continuities and discontinuities in human development.

One of the facts most often overlooked by those not immersed in gerontology is the high degree of variability in the elderly population (Heron and Chown, 1967; Riegel and Riegel, 1960). Our stereotypes, and not our data, force us into the impossible position of collectively defining, predicting the behavior of, and treating "the elderly" rather than individuals of a certain age.

There is little that the clinician already knows that a priori would not be relevant to clinical work with older persons. The developmental model may help to organize some sources of variance that may be controlling behavior. The implication of the findings that, in general, variance increases with age, is that the elderly will as individuals have as little in common as any other age group (e.g., children, adolescents). Many unpleasant phenomena (chronic illness, death) are highly correlated with old age; but much in the same way that measles and chicken pox are highly correlated with childhood.

The measurement of change is one of the knottier problems within psychometric theory (see Cronback and Furby, 1970; Harris, 1963). These problems are confounded when one attempts to measure change over long time periods as is the norm in adult life and aging. However, the interest in methodology in developmental psychology generated by Schaie's developmental model (see

Nesselroade and Reese, 1973; Buss, 1973) suggests an increase in sophistication of both research design and interpretations of developmental data.

BIOMEDICAL DATA AND BRAIN BEHAVIOR RELATIONSHIPS

Paul Weiss (1966), the developmental biologist, defined aging and development as follows:

> Development consists of a continuous series of processes of change and transformation, going on incessantly in uninterrupted sequences throughout the life-span of an individual from egg until death. In this light, the aging process appears as an integral part of the continuous process of development of an organism . . . . There is nothing in this picture of development to suggest any abrupt discontinuity, whether initiation or cessation, from which one could date the onset of aging. Growth goes on steadily, its *rate* declines gradually but not because the reproductive units become less efficient, but briefly because differentiation progressively reduces the generative components of cells and tissues into products.
>
> Conversely, cell degeneration and cell death are by no means peculiar to the older ages. They occur extensively in the embryonic stages (of development) . . . . Aging then in a biological perspective, must be regarded as basically a matter of disturbed normal relations—. . . since time magnifies the effects of critical disturbances of interactive relationships, the study of the aged will favor the discovery of such relations.

Weiss' definition of development is most useful. It integrates the aged with the young and forces critical reexamination of theoretical perspectives that see aging only in terms of static or declining processes.

In general, when a young and an older individual are compared on behavioral dimensions, the older individual does less well. Chronic brain syndrome (CBS), sadly, represents old age for most of us. However, while this frightening disease is found most often in older people, most older people do not suffer from CBS. Kay (1972) discussed the epidemiology of CBS in the aged and concluded that the traditional notion that all forms of mental illness arising in old age are due to underlying cerebral disease is no longer tenable. Vascular diseases have been implicated as causal in brain syndromes in the elderly (Obrist, 1972) as well as in EEG changes (slowing and (rhythm) (Thompson and Marsh, 1973) and changes in intellectual functioning (Wilkie and Eisdorfer, 1973). Foley (1972) provided a "laundry list" of disease entities that are often ignored in the older patient that may be accounting for the "organic brain syndrome" behaviors: (1) intoxicants such as prescription drugs and alcohol, for tolerance to medication is known to decrease with increasing age; (2) infections, cerebral as well as systemic; (3) metabolic disorders; (4) nutritional deficiencies; (5) benign intercranial tumors; and (6) sensory deprivation due to changes in the sensory apparatus with age.

Larsson, Sjorgen and Jacobsen (1963) estimated the lifetime risk of becoming demented at 2 percent. First degree relatives of those with dementia were found to have a fourfold increase in risk of becoming demented. Kay (1972) considered two competing theories of dementia: (1) the major gene theory of Larsson, Sjorgen and Jacobsen that hypothesizes a single dominant gene that might be present in about 12 percent of the population with its penetrance increasing with age, so that by the nineties about 40 percent of the carriers would be affected; and (2) the aging theory. The aging theory views dementia as "exaggerated aging" due to a gradual accumulation of senile changes in the brain—this theory implies that older people are mildly demented until some threshold is reached. Kay concluded that while the major gene theory has not been proven, current evidence does not seem to support the aging theory. Jarvik and Cohen (1973), however, reported a biobehavioral study in aging which suggests a relationship between chromosome loss and mental impairment and they conclude that genetic factors do play a role in old age.

Neurochemical and neuropathological changes in the aging brain have been reported. In chemical biomorphosis of human brain 30 to 90 years of age, Samorajski and Ordy (1972) reported significant declines in sulfur content, brain weight, and oxygen consumption, increases in DNA content in dry substances and percentage of water, and no change in lipid content. Thus, while there are well-defined changes at the cellular level, the meaning of these changes is not yet well understood. Autopsy data indicates a series of neuropathological changes in elderly patients with senile brain diseases. In autopsy studies of brains of nonsenile elderly, 75 percent of the brains were classified as lacking in senile signs (Malamud, 1972).

Older people have often been classed as "minimally brain damaged," assuming that diffuse cerebral atrophy accounted for their poorer performance (Reed and Reitan, 1963). Benton and Van Allen (1972) review the literature which indicates that the elderly often perform more like younger brain damaged patients than young normal controls. Benton and Van Allen report data from a study of their facial recognition test that shows a significant mean drop with age, but then go on to point out that the lower mean score of the old people was more a function of the failure to obtain superior scores than the obtaining of pathological score levels.

Woodruff (1973), in summarizing data on the psychophysiology of aging, reports that biological efficiency declines at about 1 percent per year from ages 30 through 80 (Chinn, 1969; DeVries, 1969; Shock, 1962) and emphasized that the rate of change is important. Birren (1963) espoused a discontinuity hypothesis in that the physiological changes are essentially benign until a critical level has been reached. However, Woodruff (1973) points out that, in a sense, physiology need not be destiny, as certain well-known physiological changes in old age may be at least partially reversible. DeVries (1969, 1970) found that regular exercise increased physiological responsiveness toward younger levels and biofeedback in alpha conditioning of the EEG was demonstrated by Woodruff (1972). Alex Comfort (1963) made the comment that, with the rise of medicine, disease has been defined as that which responds to treatment, and age changes, those things that do not.

The clinical implications of the biomedical data reviewed above are crucial for successful treatment of the aged. Often, medical care is not sought for a potentially controllable disease process in time for the intervention to have any significant ameliorative effects, as we expect older persons to show behavioral declines. It is possible that what we stoically accept as the grim picture of old age ("sans teeth, sans mind") is partially a result of our failures to intervene at a critical point. Preventive therapies need to be developed. Sudden behavioral changes need to be examined with the same set of attitudes one may typically find when a young child's behavior changes suddenly, apparently without reason. The true "causal" agents need to be sought. There is no guarantee that such an approach will "cure" the problems we typically associate with advancing age but it does seem to be the strategy that will best separate aging from disease.

CHANGES IN SENSORY SYSTEMS WITH AGE

Changes in the visual system with age are well documented, and in many cases can be remedied with corrective lenses and/or environmental modifications. Presbyopia, difficulty in focusing on near objects, is caused by a loss of elasticity in the lens. This process starts in childhood, and at about the age of 40 bifocals are generally required. There is also a decline in visual acuity after the fifth decade of life. Dark adaptation declines linearly with age from the twenties

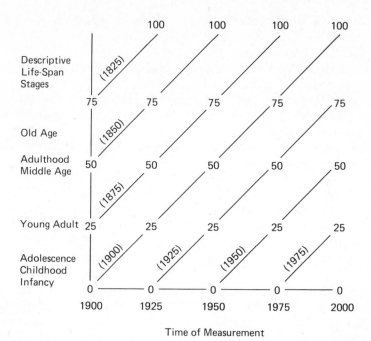

Figure 6-1.

on, with a required doubling of illumination with age due to a restriction in pupil size, as well as increased sensitivity to glare which is accelerated after age forty. As the lens yellows, color vision is also affected, primarily the shorter wave lengths (green–blue–purple). There is also a gradual shrinkage of the visual field which is slight until about age 55.

In auditory function, ability to perceive the higher frequencies declines after age 40, particularly at the higher frequencies (1,000 Hz–two octaves above middle C). Pitch discrimination and threshold may also be increased, leading to difficulties in speech discrimination. Older people have also been reported to have a more difficult time filtering speech from a noisy background. The effects of noise pollution are just now being investigated, but cross-cultural studies indicate that either noise pollution, diet, or cardiovascular disease may be implicated in what we take for granted as "normal" hearing loss in U.S. elderly (Botwinick, 1973; MacFarland, 1968).

There is little evidence on touch and vibratory sensitivity; what little there is indicated a decreased sensitivity and perhaps a decreased pain sensitivity. Changes in taste and smell have been reported in the literature as gradual. However, work in progress by

Schiffman (1973) indicates dramatically reduced taste in the elderly which she attributes mostly to changes in olfaction.

In short, it appears that there are a wide variety of changes in sensory systems with age that progress at slow stable rates from childhood on, reaching critical levels in old age. The research in this area provides a good model for dealing with age-related changes. That is, the reality of structural, irreversible deficits is accepted leading to the development of prosthetic devices and looking towards environmental manipulations that can help compensate for declining capacities.

A second point worth considering is how much capacity is really required for effective participation in our society? As we know from studies of individual differences in populations of the same age, the minimal or adequate level of functioning may be below the population average. Thus, even if an older person is operating at 50 percent of his or her peak capacity, the absolute level may still be adequate. Such an attitude might be tremendously helpful in dealing with the "fear" or dread of aging so commonly observed in middle-aged and older persons, who so often start sentences: "I just can't _____ like I used to." While such a statement is most certainly true, it needn't imply that the nursing home is around the next corner. A more rational acceptance of self might well be promoted by approach to the study of human performance and a therapeutic attitude that emphasized not the upper limits of human capacities, but rather, the necessary and sufficient behavioral components required for effective behavior

COGNITIVE FUNCTIONING: INTELLECTUAL CHANGES WITH AGE

Cognitive development has generated a tremendous and varied literature in developmental psychology, which has indicated that things are much more complex than had been thought in the past. Excellent reviews of the literature in this area have been written by Arenberg (1973); Baltes and Labouvie (1973); Bayley (1968); Botwinick (1967; 1973); Goulet and Baltes (1970); Jarvik, Eisdorfer, and Blum (1973); and Welford and Birren (1965). Thus, in this section, attention will be focused on implications of the literature for the definition of normal aging.

The study of intellectual growth and development has been a major concern of psychologists involved in aging research. Early cross-sectional studies—e.g., Jones and Conrad (1933); Miles and Miles (1932); Raven (1948); Weschler (1944, 1958); and Willoughby (1927)—indicated that I.Q. peaked at an early age (late teens, early twenties, middle thirties) as the studies were reported from the 1920s to the 1950s and then tended to decline as age approached the seventh and eighth decades of life. Verbal functions held up better than the nonverbal—e.g., problem solving and psychomotor abilities—but essentially the shapes of the curves were similar.

Then in the 1950s results of the first longitudinal studies became available (Owens, 1953; Bayley and Oden, 1955), indicating that intelligence tended to rise through young adulthood and then level off, or to increase slightly until the seventies for verbal functions and to drop off gradually after midlife for nonverbal functions.

Four major lines of research in this area can be seen as attempts to cope with the discrepancy between longitudinal cross-sectional measures of intellectual functioning:

1. Schaie's (1965) developmental model provided a major new framework for analysis of developmental data (see Figure 6-1). Kuhlen (1963) discussed the importance of cultural factors as sources of variance in developmental data for which Schaie's model provided the necessary statistical techniques. Most of the published work using sequential strategies has come from the "Schaie group" (e.g., Schaie and Strother, 1968a, 1968b) and has indicated that cohort effects control a fair amount of the variance that had been attributed to age when considering differences in intellectual performance. In concert with this approach, studies that have controlled for the amount of formal education between widely disparate age groups (e.g., Birren and Morrison, 1961; Green, 1969) have indicated that the cross-sectional descriptions of age differences in intellectual performance might be more correctly reflective of the amount of formal education in the age groups (i.e., young adults having 14 years of education, while the oldest cohorts might average five to six years of formal education).

2. A second major trend involves a consideration of the terminal drop hypothesis, which suggests that changes in performance in both longitudinal and cross-sectional studies are contaminated by terminal drops—that is, that cognitive behavior may well be stable throughout adult life until within approximately five years of death (Kleemeier, 1962; Riegel and Riegel, 1972; Wilkie and Eisdorfer, 1974), with the important theoretical notion that distance from death rather than distance from birth (chronological age) may be the critical parameter for understanding cognitive changes in the elderly (Kinsbourne and Caplan, 1973; Lieberman, 1965; Siegler, 1975). Allied with this line of thinking is the importance of dropout due to causes other than death (refusal, sickness, mobility) acting to bias the data (Siegler, 1973; Rosenthal and Rosnow, 1969).

3. Factor analytic approaches to the study of intellectual growth

and decline (e.g., Horn and Cattell, 1966) indicate that different types of functioning representing crystallized abilities, fluid abilities, and anlage capacities have different developmental histories (see Horn, 1970). Work by Blum, Clark and Jarvik (1973) on their longitudinal study of senescent twins is supportive of this theoretical work in indicating that changes in response speed may be "true ontogenetic" changes while other cognitive functions may well be contaminated by terminal drop and health status of the individual.

4. In agreement with the work cited above, observed changes in I.Q. may be more a function of health status (in particular, of cardiovascular disease) than of aging (Baer, 1972; Wilkie and Eisdorfer, 1973).

There still remain many unanswered questions about the meaning of intelligence in the aging literature. We know that, for middle class children, the I.Q. is a good predictor of school achievement, and the aging literature is beginning to indicate that I.Q. is a good predictor of survival. However, as the factor analytic approaches have shown, I.Q. is an extremely complex indicator. The diagnostic significance of the various intelligence tests for the elderly is also a open question. It would be helpful to have reliable measures of specific cognitive functions within the assessment battery for older persons. Here, the entire question of psychometric testing of older persons becomes relevant. The majority of the tests are written for younger populations, and, as with the rest of the experimental psychology literature, there are important questions as to age-appropriateness of stimuli, the proper norms, and what is the meaning of an age-fair test (there are analogous problems in defining what a culture-fair test is). Similarly the parameters of the testing situation itself (reactive measurements, experimenter bias, etc.) still need to be explored with elderly persons.

THE EXPERIMENTAL PSYCHOLOGY OF AGE DIFFERENCES

In discussing research methods in traditional psychological studies, Botwinick (1973) presents a quote from Robert Kastenbaum as a caution in interpretation of results from studies that compare disparate age groups:

> Occasionally I have the opportunity to chat with elderly people who live in the communities near Cushing Hospital. I cannot help but observe that many of these people speak with an Italian accent. I also chat with young adults who live in these same communities. They do NOT speak with an

Italian accent. As a student of human behavior and development, I am interested in this discrepancy. I indulge in some deep thinking and come up with the following conclusion: as people grow older they develop Italian accents. This must surely be one of the prime manifestations of aging on the psychological level.

Kastenbaum is making a very serious point in a delightful way. The literature in the experimental psychology of age differences in cognitive performance is large and complex, as are the problems in obtaining "comparable" groups of young and old subjects for study. Nonetheless, in general, the literature in this area consists of experimental designs where groups of young subjects (usually college students) are compared with groups of elderly subjects, who are often matched for amount of education or verbal I.Q. In general, the younger subjects are found to be faster, more efficient problem-solvers and processers of information, better able to take advantage of cues present in verbal material, less liable to interference in memory tasks, and more able to ignore irrelevant information (Botwinick, 1973; Kay, 1968; Talland, 1968). In other words, one might say that the young can play the experimenter's game (whatever it is) better than the old. The experimenter can change the game, however, such that the old perform better than the young. For example, Monge and Gardner (1972) report results from a series of vocabulary tests that were constructed decade by decade, such as a test of slang words that either entered the lexicon between 1900 and 1960 or that contained words in categories that older people were more likely to know, such as financial terms, that indicated it is possible to build tests that are "age-fair" or at least age-balanced— such that, on the item level, older populations tend to score higher than younger ones.

Other attempts have been made to construct "age-appropriate" stimuli (e.g., Arenberg, 1973) but often these involve going from a more abstract to a more concrete set of stimuli. The performance of the older groups is, in general, enhanced with the more concrete stimuli.

One important consideration in theorizing about age differences in cognitive performance is summed up in the competence-performance distinction, a term most readily identified with the psycholinguistic movement. If the differences between young and old are a competence distinction (implying that the requisite structures or functions are not present, as is often the case in very young children or in severely brain damaged individuals of any age) then there is little that a behavioral scientist can do to intervene. If, however, the differences between young and old are a performance distinction (the underlying capacity is assumed there) then the assumption is that other factors, such as motivation or CNS arousal, lack of practice with "school tasks," or choice of an inefficient strategy, to name only a few of the possible factors, then it is possible for the behavioral scientist to manipulate the experimental conditions and to try interventions designed to maximize the older person's performance.

There has been a lot of experimental work done with the assumption of performance differences which in general finds that more liberal time limits and less stressful experimental surroundings tend to reduce the differences between young and old.

Three recent studies (Denney, 1974a, 1974b; Eisdorfer, Nowlin, and Wilkie, 1970; Hoyer, Labouvie, and Baltes, 1973) suggest three different interventions. Eisdorfer, Nowlin, and Wilkie found that the introduction of a chemical blocking agent in the CNS, assumed to reduce arousal, facilitated performance on a serial learning task. Denney, using a sorting task, found that older subjects who spontaneously produced design classifications (characteristics of children under six years of age) after watching a model do the task were able to produce the analytic response characteristic of older children and adults (ages nine to 50); and Hoyer, Labouvie, and Baltes introduced nonreinforced and reinforced practice for subjects aged 60 to 85 and found improvements in the groups that had been given the training.

There has been a long literature indicating that older people are more rigid; that, once they develop a set, they will persist even if new information tells them they should change; and that, in general, the performance of older people tends to be slower and more accurate (see Botwinick, 1973: Chown, 1968; Kogan, 1973 for excellent reviews of this literature).

Wallach and Kogan (1961) indicated that when older and younger people were asked to make decisions about life situations, older people were more cautious than younger people. Botwinick (1966) used the same life situations as Wallach and Kogan but added a second set of life situations with elderly protagonists. While the older subjects were more cautious than the younger ones, Botwinick's results also showed that both young and old were more conservative regarding the younger protagonists than the older protagonists.

Botwinick (1969) replicated the 1966 study leaving out the most conservative alternative. Under these conditions, no age differences were found, and Botwinick concluded that the cautiousness observed in the elderly was due to their avoidance of risk situations. However, if the risk could not be avoided, the elderly's decisions were not different from the young. Cautiousness and rigidity in the elderly have often been seen as serving realistic needs of conserving energy, and simplifying the world in adaptive attempts to cope with declining capacities. Botwinick's (1969) results indicate that perhaps the frame of reference or world view is different, leading to preferred cognitive modes.

Another approach in the study of cognitive behavior is the structuralist viewpoint represented by Piaget (1972). In essence, the Piagetian approach to cognitive development attempts to specify the development of cognitive behavior after adolescence. He suggests that formal operations may get tied to occupational roles and thus expressed within the rubric of the adult's normal life space, or that alternatively there is a diversification of aptitudes in adult cognition. Flavell (1970) commented on adult cognition from a Piagetian perspective, and emphasized that cognitive growth in adult life is quantitatively different from what is observed in childhood. The large reorganizations of thought that define each of the Piagetian stages in childhood are absent in adulthood. Second, biological growth is happening at such a slow rate that perhaps the study of adult cognition is the "nearest thing we have to a pure experiment in nature for assessing the change making power of experience alone." Experiential aspects of adult life certainly change at a faster rate than the biological functions we are able to measure; it is certainly not the case, that the organism ceases to develop in a psychobiological way after adolescence.

Riegel (1973) rejected the Piagetian model as inappropriate to the study of adult cognition. He proposes a dialectic model that incorporates what Riegel feels is the most important aspect of adult cognition—the ability to recognize and simultaneously deal with the contradictions in life. Riegel postulates a dialectic continuation of each of the four Piagetian stages that the adult uses where appropriate (sensory-motor while making love, representational while appreciating art, concrete-operational while carrying out most of life's daily routine tasks, and formal-operational while theorizing). Riegel's position is not really in conflict with Piaget's earlier writing on the transition from adolescence to adulthood (Inhelder and Piaget, 1958).

In the final chapter of their book on adolescent cognition, Inhelder and Piaget introduce the affective dimension into the cognitive structure of the adolescent. The mechanism of egocentrism in adolescence is essentially the same mechanism as is used earlier in development; but for the adolescent the task is to adapt his ego to the full social environment, including work and adult responsibilities. The "egocentric" adolescent conflict or confusion comes from the fact that the adolescent, instead, attempts to adapt the world to his ego.

With formal operations the adolescent, for the first time, gains the capacity to think about thought. Inhelder and Piaget (1958) note:

> We are struck by the fact that the feeling about ideals is practically non-existent in the child ... it is only during adolescence with the development of formal structures that ideas become autonomous. Thus to say that adolescence is the age at which adolescents take their place in adult society is ... to maintain that it is the age of formation of the personality, for the adoption of adult roles is from another and necessarily complementary standpoint, the construction of a personality.

The literature in cognitive development is perhaps the richest and most confusing. When life space comparisons are made in cross-sectional studies, it is often noticed that the older group's performance is at the level achieved during middle childhood. Structuralist perspectives force our attention to a consideration of the underlying causes of such apparent similarities in behavior. It seems likely that factors such as motivation, personality, educational history, reactions to the experimental situation, and other non-cognitive factors may be responsible for many of the performance deficits in the elderly. On the other side, neuropsychological and physiological research is starting to investigate the competence that can reasonably be expected from an aging nervous system.

At present, it seems fair to say that older individuals performance on cognitive tasks is modifiable, and that, in general, in tasks where speed is an important component of performance, older people will do less well. Research in the structuralist tradition indicates that the organization of cognitive functions may be different in older individuals.

The theoretical perspective of the researcher-clinician is also crucial in this important area. The implications of a deficit versus a compensatory model of functioning are tremendous. As this cursory review has shown, it is possible to design experiments that both minimize and maximize elderly individuals' performance. The problem of deciding on the appropriate criterion or standard of behavior is perhaps clearest in terms of cognitive performance. For example, if mandatory retirement policies were based solely on performance criteria, it would be possible to design instruments to measure the required capacities, and also to design and modify the requirements of the task. Yet current economic conditions and social policies tend to ignore individual capacities. Experimental work in middle and old age has only recently gone beyond the descriptive studies and started asking important questions about what accounts for the observed performance differences. To the extent that cohort differences have been shown to be important, it is interesting to speculate that, as future generations age, they may have more in common with themselves at younger ages than with the elderly of today.

PERSONALITY, MOTIVATION, AND ADJUSTMENT

The literature in this area is richer in theory than in data. It is important to keep in mind the potential danger of building a descriptive theory of personality and adjustment, for it might lead to an "institutionalization" of patterns of adjustment as "normal" that reflects more about the responses of specific cohorts to cultural pressures—the "performance" aspects of personality rather than the "competence" aspects of personality.

Perhaps the most influential data set in the adult personality area stems from the Kansas City Studies of Adult Life (Cumming and Henry, 1961), which proposed the "disengagement" theory—simply stated, in old age there appears to be a mutual disengagement of the individual from society as well as of society from the individual, leading to good adjustment (measured as high morale) being associated with a decrease in engagement (measured as social interaction). This led to an opposing view, which has been labeled "activity" theory, that postulates high morale associated with high social interaction. Disengagement theory proved to be of enormous significance because of its heuristic value. The research generated both in sociology and in psychology has been fruitful. Briefly, in work that followed similar studies by Reichard, Livson, and Peterson (1962) and Havighurst, Neugarten, and Tobin (1968) produced factor analytic typologies that allowed for various styles of adjustment that related to various life satisfaction indices. Continuity was seen as an important mediator, as was the attitude the person had both about his life at the current moment and about the evaluation of his past life. The work of the Chicago group has been most productive and can be found in volumes edited by Neugarten (1964, 1968) and in her review papers (1969, 1973). Issues that have been considered by this group of investigators have included a consideration of Erikson's eight stages of man model—with a finer grain analysis of the adult and old age stages which essentially suggest that shifts need to be made from active, physical participation to a valuing mind over body, and valuing thought and investment in the active future of younger generations (Gruen, 1964; Peck, 1968; Peck and Berkowitz, 1964).

Work by Neugarten and Gutmann (1964) on the TAT indicated shifts with increasing age from active to passive to magical styles of mastery. Gutmann (1968) has also shown this to be a phenomenon generalizable to other cultures. Questions of timing of life and the importance of being "on" or "off" time in major life events (Neugarten, 1969), the age-status-structure of our society (Neugarten and Moore, 1968), as well as the changing roles of men and women within the family have also been shown to be important factors. Neugarten and Gutmann (1964) used a specially constructed TAT card that portrayed a two generation family of adult children with elderly parents. The older female was seen as increasing in dominance and power while the older male was seen in softer, more affiliative, terms.

From a sociocultural perspective, the classes of people labeled "adolescent" and "aged" share similar positions: neither is in the mainstream of power, both groups may be struggling to gain/ maintain independence, gain/maintain financial security, gain/main-tain employment, and so on. Looft (1973) reviewed the literature on socialization and referred to some of his data on age perception. He found that middle-aged people were correctly perceived by both young and old age groups. The interest in age perception is relatively recent and should prove to be fascinating.

Socialization may also be seen as a life span process (Brim and Wheeler, 1966). In childhood the parents are the primary socializers, with peers second. Peers probably overtake parents sometime later on, and I would assume that the majority of adult socialization is done by peers. Yet the elderly have a problem, often, in finding a peer group that they both have proximity to and wish to identify with. Attachment is a term we usually associate only with mother-infant interaction, and then mainly from the perspective of the infant (Hartup and Lempers, 1973) yet "attachment" may grow up to be intimacy, which is a crucial variable in adult life (see Lowenthal and Haven, 1968; Lowenthal and Chiriboga, 1973).

Kuhlen's (1968) view of motivation across the life span and Lawton's ecological approach (Lawton and Nahemow, 1973) repre-sent two approaches that help organize the issues in this complex area.

Kuhlen postulated two major trends in adult life: a continued need for growth and expansion, and an increasing susceptibility to threat with increasing age. The influence of the ego psychologists such as Charlotte Buhler (see Buhler and Massarik, 1968) is felt, as is the influence of Kurt Lewin. Kuhlen suggests that Murray's need-press framework is useful for understanding changes across the life span. Briefly, in this model the need is defined as a characteristic of the individual, the press as a need satisfied that is a characteristic of the environment (broadly defined to include almost all outside of the person). The individual with a need must choose a press (alpha-direct, or beta-vicarious), then will experience some degree of satisfaction (0 percent to 100 percent), and must then adjust to the situation he has created. Maslow's (1954) hierarchy of needs, which start with needs for basic food, shelter, safety—and end up with needs for self-actualization, aesthetics, etc., represents a fair sampling of human needs. Kuhlen's point is that needs are operative unless they have been satisfied or, if chronically unsatisfied, they will drop out. As the individual ages, he may work through the need hierarchy until unexpected changes such as retirement, loss of spouse, etc. may bring some of the early needs back into operation later in life. A second major point is that the available presses in the environment may also change with age. While a majority of Kuhlen's concerns were aimed at the "person," the majority of Lawton's concerns rest with the "environment." In their "ecological theory of adaptive behavior and aging," Lawton and Nahemow (1973) defined five major components of their transactional model: (1) degree of individual competence; (2) environmental press; (3) adaptive behavior; (4) affective responses; and (5) adaptation level. Lawton suggests that the environment may be more malleable than the individual in old age, thus that is a potentially productive place for us to put our energies.

Negative attitudes and stereotypes about old people have been discussed by the other authors in this volume and have been recently reviewed by Bennett and Eckman (1973). The concept of "age-ism" has begun to attract attention in the media and public consciousness. It is perhaps more serious that age-ism exists within psychology, and majority of the health-care professions. A key problem in the entire area of gerontology was summed up by June Blum (see Chapter Eight)—the problem of empathy. For most of us, *regardless of age*, "the elderly are them." A life span developmental perspective can provide an integrative context for evaluation and treatment of the elderly.

Many of the problems of aging are problems of poverty, chronic disease, unemployment, widowhood, etc. These problems are not the exclusive property of the elderly, and remedies proven effective for younger populations may also prove effective for older persons. Often, what is unique about the elderly, is not *the* problem; rather, there are multiple problems, and many of the resources available to younger persons (through jobs, family members) are not available to older persons. An approach that emphasizes individual differences and looks for strengths and weaknesses of both the individual and the environment, as well as toward established knowledge bases, with an eye toward the relevant modification, should provide a rich base for the creation of a clinical psychology of aging.

REFERENCES

Arenberg, D. Cognition and aging: Verbal learning, memory and problem solving. In C. Eisdorfer and M.P. Lawton, eds., *The psychology of adult development and aging.* Washington, D.C.: American Psychological Association, 1973.

Baer, P.E. Cognitive changes in aging. In C.M. Gaitz, ed., *Aging and the brain.* New York: Plenum Press, 1972.

Baltes, P.B. and Labouvie, G.V. Adult development of intellectual performance: Description, explanation and modification. In C. Eisdoerfer and M.P. Lawton, eds., *The psychology of adult development and aging.* Washington, D.C.: American Psychological Association, 1973.

Baltes, P.B.; Schaie, K.W.; and Nardi, A.H. Age and experimental mortality in a seven-year longitudinal study of cognitive behavior. *Developmental Psychology,* 1971, *5:* 18-26.

Bayley, N. Cognition and aging. In K.W. Schaie, ed., *Theory and methods of research in aging.* Morgantown: West Virginia University, 1968.

Bayley, N. and Oden, M.H. The maintenance of intellectual ability in gifted adults. *Journal of Gerontology,* 1955, *10:* 91-107.

Bennett, R. and Eckman, J. Attitudes toward aging: A critical examination of recent literature and implications for future research. In C. Eisdorfer and M.P. Lawton, eds., *The psychology of adult development and aging.* Washington, D.C.: American Psychological Association, 1973.

Benton, A.L. and Van Allen, M.W. Aspects of neuropsychological assessment in patients with cerebral disease. In C.M. Gaitz, ed., *Aging and the brain.* New York: Plenum Press, 1972.

Birren, J.E. Psychophysiological relations. In J.E. Birren, R.N. Butler, S.W. Greenhouse, L. Sokoloff, and M.R. Yarrow, eds., *Human aging: A biological and behavioral study.* Washington, D.C.: United States Government Printing Office, 1963.

Birren, J.E. and Morrison, D.F. Analysis of the WAIS subtests in relation to age and education. *Journal of Gerontology,* 1961, *16:* 363-369.

Birren, J.E. and Woodruff, D.S. Academic and professional training in the psychology of aging. In C. Eisdorfer and M.P. Lawton, eds., *The psychology of adult development and aging.* Washington, D.C.: American Psychological Association, 1973.

Blum, J.E.; Clark, E.T.; and Jarvik, L.F. The New York State Psychiatric Institute study of aging twins. In L.F. Jarvik, C. Eisdorfer, and J.E. Blum, eds., *Intellectual functioning in adults.* New York: Springer Publishing Co., 1973.

Botwinick, J. Cautioness in advanced age. *Journal of Gerontology*, 1966, *21:* 347-353.

———. *Cognitive process in maturity and old age.* New York: Springer Publishing Co., 1967.

———. Disinclination to venture response vs. cautioness in responding: Age differences. *Journal of Genetic Psychology*, 1969, *115:* 55-62.

———. *Aging and behavior.* New York: Springer Publishing Co. 1973.

Brim, O.G. and Wheeler, S. *Socialization after childhood.* New York: John Wiley and Sons, 1966.

Buss, A.R. An extension of developmental models that separate ontogenetic changes and cohort differences. *Phychological Bulletin*, 1973, *80:* 466-79.

Buhler, C. and Massarik, F., eds. *The course of human life.* New York: Springer Publishing Co.., 1968.

Chinn, A.B. Physiology of human aging. In J.E. Birren, ed., *Contemporary gerontology: Concepts and issues.* Los Angeles: Andrus Gerontology Center, 1969.

Chown, S.M. Personality and aging. In K.W. Schaie, ed., *Theory and methods of research in aging.* Morgantown: West Virginia University, 1968.

Comfort, A. *The biology of senescence.* New York; Holt, Rinehart & Winston, Inc., 1973.

———. Biological theories of aging. *Human Development*, 1970, *13:* 127-39.

Cronbach, L.J. and Furby, L. How should we measure "change"—or should we? *Psychological Bulletin*, 1970, *74:* 68-80.

Cumming, M.E. and Henry, W. *Growing old.* New York: Basic Books, 1961.

Denney, N.W. Classification abilities in the elderly. *Journal of Gerontology*, 1974a, *29:* 309-14.

———. Evidence for developmental changes in categorization criteria for children and adults. *Human Development*, 1974b, *17:* 41-53.

DeVries, H. Physiology of exercise and aging. In J.E. Birren, ed., *Contemporary gerontology: Concepts and issues.* Los Angeles: Andrus Gerontology Center, 1969.

———. Physiological effects of an exercise training regimen upon men aged 52 to 88. *Journal of Gerontology*, 1970, *25:* 325-36.

Eisdorfer, C.; Nowlin, J.B.; and Wilkie, F. Improvement of learning in the aged by modification of autonomic nervous system activity. *Science*, 1970, *170:* 1327-29.

Eisdorfer, C. and Wilkie, F. Intellectual changes with advancing age. In L.F. Jarvik, C. Eisdorfer, and J.E. Blum, eds. *Intellectual functioning in adults.* New York: Springer, 1973, 21-9.

Erikson, E.H. Identity and the life cycle. *Psychological Issues*, 1959, *1*, Monograph 1, 1-171.

Flavell, J.H. Cognitive changes in adulthood, In L.R. Goulet and P.B. Baltes, eds., *Lifespan developmental psychology: Research and theory.* New York: Academic Press, 1970.

Foley, J.M. Differential diagnosis of the organic mental disorders in elderly patients. In C.M. Gaitz, ed., *Aging and the brain.* New York: Plenum Press, 1972.

Goulet, L.R. and Baltes, P.B. eds. *Lifespan development psychology: Research and theory.* New York: Academic Press, 1970.

Green, R.F. Age-intelligence relationship between the ages of sixteen and sixty-four: A rising trend. *Developmental Psychology,* 1969, *1:* 618-27.

Gruen, W. Adult personality: An empirical study of Erikson's theory of ego-development. In B.L. Neugarten et al., eds., *Personality in middle and late life.* New York: Atherton Press, 1964.

Gurland, B.J. A broad clinical assessment of psychopathology in the aged. In C. Eisdorfer and M.P. Lawton, eds., *The psychology of adult development and aging.* Washington, D.C.: American Psychological Association, 1973.

Gutmann, D.L. Aging among the highland Maya: a comparative study. In B.L. Neugarten, ed., *Middle age and aging.* Chicago: University of Chicago Press, 1968, 444-52.

Harris, C.W. ed. *Problems in measuring change.* Madison: University of Wisconsin Press, 1963.

Hartup, W.W. and Lempers, J. A problem in lifespan development: the interactional analysis of family attachments. In P. Baltes and K.W. Schaie, eds., *Lifespan developmental psychology: personality and socialization.* New York: Academic Press, 1973, 235-52.

Havighurst, R.J.; Neugarten, B.L.; & Tobin, S.S. Disengagement and patterns of aging. In B.L. Neugarten, ed., *Middle age and aging: A reader in social psychology.* Chicago: University of Chicago Press, 1968.

Heron, A. and Chown, S. *Age and function.* London: J.A. Churchill, 1967.

Horn, J.L. Organization of lifespan data on human abilities. In L.R. Goulet and P.B. Baltes, eds., *Lifespan developmental psychology: Research and theory.* New York: Academic Press, 1970.

Horn, J.L. and Cattell, R.B. Age differences in primary mental ability factors. *Journal of Gerontology,* 1966, *21:* 210-20.

Hoyer, W.J.; Labouvie, G.V.; and Baltes, P.B. Modification of response speed deficits and intellectual performance in the elderly. *Human Development,* 1973, *13:* 233-42.

Inhelder, B. and Piaget, J. *The growth of logical thinking from childhood to adolescence.* New York: Basic Books, 1958.

Jarvik, L.F. and Cohen, D. A biobehavioral approach to intellectual change with aging. In C. Eisdorfer and M.P. Lawton, eds., *The psychology of adult development and aging.* Washington, D.C.: American Psychological Association, 1973.

Jarvik, L.F.; Eisdorfer, C.; & Blum, J.E. eds. *Intellectural functioning in adults.* New York: Springer Publishing Co., 1973

Jones, H.E. and Conrad, H.S. The growth and decline of intelligence: A study of homogenous populations between the ages of ten and sixty. *Genetic Psychology Monographs,* 1933, *13:* 233-98.

Kay, D.W.K. Epidemological aspects of organic brain disease in the aged. In C.M. Gaitz, ed., *Aging and the brain.* New York: Plenum Press, 1972.

Kay, H. Learning and aging. In K.W. Schaie, ed., *Theory and methods of research in aging.* Morgantown: West Virginia University, 1968.

Kinsbourne, M. and Caplan, P. Symposium discussion: Lifespan development of psychological aging. In P.B. Baltes, ed., Lifespan models of psychological aging: A white elephant? *The Gerontologist*, 1973, *13:* 457–512.

Kleemeier, R.W. Intellectual changes in the senium. *Proceedings of the American Statistical Association*, 1962, *1:* 290–95.

Kogan, N. Creativity and cognitive style: A lifespan perspective In P.B. Baltes and K.W. Schaie, eds., *Lifespan developmental psychology: Personality and socialization*. New York: Academic Press, 1973.

Kuhlen, R.G. Age and intelligence: The significance of cultural change in longitudinal vs. cross-sectional findings. *Vita Humana*, 1963, *6:* 113–24.

——. Developmental changes with motivation during the adult years. In B.L. Neugarten, ed., *Middle age and aging: A reader in social psychology*. Chicago: University of Chicago Press, 1968.

Larsson, T., Sjogren, T., & Jacobson, G. Senile dementia. *Acta Psychiatric Scandinavica*, 1963, *39*, Supplement 167.

Lawton, M.P. Clinical psychology? In C. Eisdorfer and M.P. Lawton, eds., *The psychology of adult development and aging*. Washington, D.C.: American Psychological Association, 1973.

Lawton, M.P. and Nahemow, L. Ecology and the aging process. In C. Eisdorfer and M.P. Lawton, eds., *The psychology of adult development and aging*. Washington, D.C.: American Psychological Association, 1973.

Lieberman, M.A. Psychological correlates of impending death: Some preliminary observations. *Journal of Gerontology*, 1965, *20:* 181–90.

Looft, W.R. Socialization in a lifespan perspective: White elephant, worms and will-o-the-wisps. In P.B. Baltes, ed., Lifespan models of psychological aging: A white elephant? *The Gerontologist*, 1973, *13:* 457–512.

Lowenthal, M.F. and Chiriboga, D. Social stress and adaptation: Toward a life course perspective. In C. Eisdorfer and M.P. Lawton, eds., *The psychology of adult development and aging*. Washington, D.C.: American Psychological Association, 1973.

Lowenthal, M.F. and Haven, C. Interaction and adaptation: Intimacy as a critical variable. In B.L. Neugarten, ed., *Middle age and aging: A reader in social psychology*. Chicago: University of Chicago Press, 1968.

MacFarland, R.A. The sensory and perceptual processes in aging. In K.W. Schaie, ed., *Theory and methods of research in aging*. Morgantown: West Virginia University, 1968.

Malamud, N. Neuropathology of organic brain syndromes associated with aging. In C.M. Gaitz, ed., *Aging and the brain*. New York: Plenum Press, 1972.

Maslow, A. *Motivation and personality*. New York: Harper and Row, 1954.

Miles, C.C. and Miles, W.R. The correlation of intelligence scores and chronological age from early to late maturity. *American Journal of Psychology*, 1932, *44:* 44–78.

Monge, R.H. and Gardner, E.F. A program of research in adult differences in cognitive performance and learning: Backgrounds for adult education and vocational retraining. U.S. Office of Education, Department of H. E. and W., January 1972.

Nesselroade, J.R. and Reese, H.W. *Lifespan developmental psychology: methodological issues*. New York: Academic Press, 1973.

Nesselroade, J.R.; Schaie, K.W.; and Baltes, P.B. Ontogenetic and generational components of structure and quantitative change in adult cognitive behavior. *Journal of Gerontology*, 1972, *27:* 222-28.

Neugarten, B.L., ed. *Middle age and aging: A reader in social psychology.* Chicago: University of Chicago Press, 1968.

———. Continuities and discontinuities of psychological issues in adult life. *Human Development*, 1969, *9:* 121-30.

———. Personality change in late life: A developmental perspective. In C. Eisdorfer and M.P. Lawton, eds., *The psychology of adult development and aging.* Washington, D.C.: American Psychological Association, 1973.

Neugarten, B.L. et al., eds. *Personality in Middle and Late Life.* New York: Atherton Press, 1964.

Neugarten, B.L. et al., eds. *Personality in middle and late life.* New York: age: A TAT study. In B.L. Neugarten et al., eds., *Personality in middle and late life.* New York: Atherton Press, 1964.

Neugarten, B.L. and Moore, J.W. The changing age status system. In B.L. Neugarten, ed., *Middle age and aging: A reader in social psychology.* Chicago: University of Chicago Press, 1968.

Obrist, W.D. Cerebral physiology of the aged: Influences of circulatory disorders. In C.M. Gaitz, ed., *Aging and the brain.* New York: Plenum Press, 1972.

Owens, W.A. Age and mental abilities: A longitudinal study. *Genetic Psychology Monographs*, 1953, *48:* 3-54.

Peck, R.C. Psychological developments in the second half of life. In B.L. Neugarten, ed., *Middle age and aging: A reader in social psychology.* Chicago: University of Chicago Press, 1968.

Peck, R.C. and Berkowitz, H. Personality and adjustment in middle age. In B.L. Neugarten et al., eds., *Personality in middle and late life.* New York: Atherton Press, 1964.

Piaget, J. Intellectual evolution from adolescence to adulthood. *Human Development*, 1972, *15:* 1-12.

Raven, J.C. The comparative assessment of intellectual ability. *British Journal of Psychology*, 1948, *39:* 12-19.

Reed, H.B.C. and Reitan, R.M. A comparison of the effects of the normal aging process with effects of organic brain damage and adaptive abilities. *Journal of Gerontology*, 1963, *18:* 177-79.

Reichard, S.; Livson, F.; and Peterson, P.G. *Aging and personality.* New York: John Wiley and Sons, 1962.

Riegel, K.F. Dialectic operations: The final period of cognitive development. *Human Development*, 1973, *16:* 346-70.

Riegel, K.F. and Riegel, R.M. A study of change of attitudes and interests during the later years of life. *Vita Humana*, 1960, *3:* 177-206.

———. Development, drop, death. *Developmental Psychology*, 1972, *6:* 306-309.

Rosenthal, R. and Rosnow, R.L. *Artifact in behavioral research.* New York: Academic Press, 1969.

Samorajski, T. & Ordy, J.M. Neurochemistry of aging. In C.M. Gaitz ed., *Aging and the brain.* New York: Plenum, 1972, 41-61.

Schaie, K.W. A general model for the study of developmental problems. *Psychological Bulletin*, 1965, *64:* 92-108.

Schaie, K.W. and Strother, C.R. Cognitive and personality variables in college graduates of advanced age. In G.A. Talland, ed., *Human aging and behavior.* New York: Academic Press, 1968a.

———. The effects of time and cohort differences on the interpretation of age changes in cognitive behavior. *Multivariate Behavioral Research*, 1968b, *3:* 258-94.

Schiffman, S.S. The dietary rehabilitation clinic: A multi-aspect dietary and behavioral approach to the treatment of obesity. Paper presented at the meetings of the Association for the Advancement of Behavior Therapy, Miami Beach, 1973.

Shock, N. The physiology of aging. *Scientific American*, 1962, *206:* 100-10.

Siegler, I.C. Threats to external validity: The effects of selective dropout on health, morale, social relations and environmental circumstances in the elderly. Doctoral dissertation, Syracuse University, 1973.

———. The terminal drop hypothesis: factor artifact. *Experimental Aging Research*, 1975, *1*, 169-85.

Talland, G.A. *Human Aging and behavior.* New York: Academic Press, 1968.

Thompson, L.W. and Marsh, G.R. Psychophysiological studies of aging. In C. Eisdorfer and M.P. Lawton, eds., *The psychology of adult development and aging.* Washington, D.C.: American Psychological Association, 1973.

Wallach, M.A. and Kogan, N. Aspects of judgement and decision making: Interrelationships and changes with age. *Behavioral Science*, 1961, *6:* 23-26.

Wechsler, D. *The Measurement of adult intelligence.* Baltimore: Williams & Wilkins Company, 1944.

———. *The measurement and appraisal of adult intelligence.* Baltimore: Williams & Wilkins Company, 1958.

Weiss, P. Aging: A corollary of development. In N.W. Shock, ed., *Perspectives in experimental gerontology.* Springfield, Ill.: Charles C. Thomas, 1966.

Welford, A.T. and Birren, J.E. *Behavior, aging and the nervous system.* Springfield, Ill.: Charles C. Thomas, 1965.

Wilkie, F. and Eisdorfer, C. Systemic disease and behavioral correlates. In L.F. Jarvik, C. Eisdorfer, and J.E. Blum eds., *Intellectual functioning in adults.* New York: Spring Publishing, 1973, 83-93.

———. Terminal changes in intelligence. In E. Palmore ed., *Normal aging II.* Durham, N.C.: Duke University Press, 1974, 103-15.

Willoughby, R.R. Family similarities in mental test abilities. *Genetic Psychology Monographs*, 1927, *2:* 235-77.

Woodruff, D.S. Biofeedback control of EEG alpha rhythm and effect on reaction time in young and old. Doctoral dissertation, University of Southern California, 1972.

———. The usefulness of lifespan approach to the psychophysiology of aging. In P.B. Baltes, ed., Lifespan models of psychological aging: A white elephant? *The Gerontologist*, 1973, *13:* 457-512.

Chapter 7

Community Geropsychology: Issues of Training and Service*

Margaret Gatz, Dan Hurley, and
Gurudershan Singh Nagel
University of Maryland

This chapter is addressed to defining, assessing, and integrating the concepts of gerontology and community psychology, and to exploring the implications of a community geropsychology model for training and service. This chapter attempts, first, to assess the present state of development of each of the concepts separately—geropsychology, community psychology, and training—and, second, to propose an intervention model that integrates the current strengths of each of these components.

The conference on which this chapter is based reflects a sudden upsurge of interest in the mental health and other problems of the aged in America. The recent establishment of a National Institute on Aging also reflects the trend. Moreover, the government report concerning the Research on Aging Act (1973) states that "basic research in the process of aging is widely recognized in the scientific community as an idea whose time has come." These facts suggest the beginning of a dramatic shift in priorities. The aged have very much

*This chapter was jointly prepared by a faculty member, M. Gatz, and two graduate students, D. Hurley and G.S. Nagel, from the University of Maryland Clinical-Community Psychology Program, for presentation June 14, 1974, at the geropsychology conference sponsored by the Duke University Center for the Study of Aging and Human Development. The proposed community geropsychology training and service model has grown out of the efforts of not only the authors, but also the director of clinical training, Forrest B. Tyler, and other members of the University of Maryland Clinical Psychology Training Program, in attempting to develop a community-related program of training and service in Prince Georges County, Maryland. The authors also would like to thank Dr. Tyler for critically reading this manuscript.

constituted a neglected minority. The culture, as the Gray Panthers and others have pointed out, promotes routine neglect of the elderly, and other practices that discriminate against the aged. Nor has the field of psychology been particularly involved in either research or applied clinical work with the aging. The small contingent of professionals who have been most concerned with caring for the mental health of the elderly, with planning and evaluating programs, and with understanding the aging process have generally been from the fields of medicine, psychiatry, social work, sociology, and nursing.

This apparent disregard for the mental health problems of the older person does not reflect a lower prevalence of such problems in that age bracket. Quite the contrary. Cross-sectional statistics suggest at least a fourfold increase in significant mental or emotional illness, particularly psychotic symptomatology and suicide, in persons past age 65 as compared to younger persons (Dohrenwend and Dohren-wend, 1969; Kramer, Taube, and Redick, 1973). The treatment facilities most widely used by this older population are the mental hospitals. While approximately one in ten persons is in the age group 65 years and older, approximately half of patient care episodes in state and county mental hospitals are accounted for by patients aged 65 and older (Kramer, Taube, and Redick, 1973). It should be noted that aged mental patients include both patients who were hospital-ized at a younger age and grew old in the hospital and patients whose first contact with the mental health system occured in old age. In the past 20 years, admissions to mental hospitals have declined, and nursing homes have begun to provide predominantly custodial care to many aged who would previously have been hospitalized. In contrast, mental health clinics and private psychiatric outpatient services are dramatically underused by the aging. Persons aged 65 and above constitute 2 percent of the typical caseload of outpatient psychiatric services, 1 percent of admissions to daycare services, and 4 percent of admissions to community mental health center services (Eisdorfer, 1972; Kramer, Taube, and Redick, 1973). The com-munity mental health center has tended to omit the aging from its prevention and outreach efforts. In the 1966 American Psychological Association position statement on community mental health centers, Smith and Hobbs wrote about the necessity of giving some attention to "planning for problem groups that nobody wants . . . .. There are a number of such groups of people, among whom problems of human ineffectiveness are obvious, yet whose difficulties cannot accurately or helpfully be described as mainly psychological; for example, addicts, alcoholics, the aging, delinquents, the mentally retarded."

Thus, the present climate might be summarized as follows: there has long been a pattern of disregard of the aging by psychologists and other mental health workers, and now suddenly older persons are beginning to constitute one of the new major foci of the mental health effort in this country. These shifting priorities would seem to demand that geropsychology not respond haphazardly, as if to the newest fad, but that it should involve itself in self-examination and in the generation of viable and effective models of training and service.

GEROPSYCHOLOGY

Let us begin such a self-examination with the geropsychology component of the community geropsychology training and service model. To date there has been really no such geropsychology component; that is, there is no integrated body of substance, theory, applications, and methodology addressed to or explicitly including the aging and the mental health problems of the aging. In the 1973 book from the American Psychological Association Task Force on Aging, Eisdorfer and Lawton reached a similar conclusion, stating bluntly that "the fact is that there is no clinical psychology of old age," and suggesting that the lack of attention by theorists to the psychodynamics of the aging personality may be a concomitant phenomenon. In the same book, Neugarten (1973) pointed out that data and an accompanying conceptual framework that would address personality processes through the life cycle are still minimal. We have already described the neglect of the aged by professionals engaged in the delivery of mental health services.

In defining geropsychology today it seems important to draw upon the strengths and the current directions of both gerontology and the profession of clinical psychology. Five aspects that seem particularly relevant to explaining aging behavior are a life-span developmental perspective, conceptions of positive mental health, an interdisciplinary focus of research and practice, and an emphasis on social and environmental factors. Let us elaborate on each of these elements in turn.

The first is the trend toward conceptualizing in terms of *life span* or *life cycle*. Behavior patterns are best understood within their developmental context. Thus, formulating what a person is about entails considering a developmental sequence, including both past and future, which bears on present functioning. Similar behaviors (e.g., driving a car, taking an I.Q. test, threatening suicide) may actually constitute very different events for people at different times during the life cycle. A life span developmental perspective additionally leads to a conceptualization of life as involving a series of "developmental tasks" (Havighurst, 1972), e.g., beginning school, going off to college, developing a life's work, having children, retirement, death. The notion of a developmental task "assumes an active learner interacting with an active social environment" (Havighurst, 1972). Each person evolves individual styles of coping with these tasks. Individual psychosocial competence would then be defined in terms of one's success in handling these developmental tasks. A life span perspective, by emphasizing that development is a human process, and by recognizing that people of any age have needs, hopes, fears, and ways of coping with them, grants dignity and personhood to people, old and young.

The second element that we considered important in defining geropsychology, conceptions of *positive mental health*, involves moving beyond traditional definitions of mental health and illness to the establishment of criteria of effective functioning, and moving beyond merely treating the mentally ill to developing ways to foster increased effectiveness in all people. One implication for psychological intervention with the aged in particular is the emphasis on what people can do, on their competencies, not on what they cannot do. This orientation leads to the development of programs that help and encourage people to function to the extent to which they are able and that maximize the opportunities for competent functioning. The concept of positive mental health is related to such notions as successfully coping with developmental tasks, "life-satisfaction" (Neugarten, 1974), "successful aging" (Pfeiffer, 1974), and perception of well-being (Chiriboga, 1974).

A third important element is the current *multidisciplinary* status of gerontology. Many research and training programs in aging, such as the Duke University Center for the Study of Aging and Human Development, include professionals from many disciplines—medical science, social science, political science—and encourage interaction among the disciplines. It is to be hoped that a geropsychology will preserve an openness to perspectives and concepts from other disciplines and will continue to encourage interdisciplinary interaction and cooperation both in university programs and within and among service agencies.

A fourth aspect is the *interrelationship of research and practice*. Kent, Kastenbaum, and Sherwood (1972) made the assessment that the young and multidisciplinary nature of the field of gerontology permits and encourages an action-research approach. Their book is the first survey of implementation of this model in gerontology. Thus, in formulating a geropsychology, it may be helpful to draw upon scientist-professional models developed by clinical psychology, which address the action-research integration and the training of people for scientist-professional roles.

The final current direction that is important to consider in building a geropsychology is the emphasis on *social factors* as important explanatory variables. Gottesman, Quarterman, and Cohn (1973) have discussed the aging person's behavior as a function of his abilities and of his expectancies of himself, the immediate group, and the society. The model proposed by Schaie (1970) in his research on intelligence sorts out the role of cultural, historical, and selectivity factors from the effects of aging. Lawton (1973), in his discussion of the ecology of aging, has created a two factor model based on individual competence and environmental demands. It has been argued by James (1964), for example, that our society is organized almost as though we are contriving to create rather than to prevent mental illness in older people. We do this by retiring and isolating older people and denying them activities or roles that would make them feel useful or needed. Further, the tendency, with older people especially, has been toward institutionalization rather than community-based treatment. A survey of resource allocation to various programs will demonstrate that institutionalization is encouraged by the allocation of few resources to support older people in the community (Taber and Flynn, 1971).

In terms of implications for intervention, then, change must be conceived of in terms of these social variables and in terms of establishing programs that operate on and within the individual–social system matrix. Thus, a comprehensive geropsychology seems to require for its basis an integrative model such as that of community psychology.

COMMUNITY PSYCHOLOGY

Faced with shortages of manpower and reports of nonexistent or ineffective service delivery to large segments of society, the mental health system in general, and clinical psychology in particular, have begun to develop alternative models of mental health. Cowen (1973) provides a summary of both the need and the call for an alternative paradigm.

However understandable the evolution and ascendance of the medical model, however necessary that portions of it survive, however much we can improve its efficiency, it fails to deal satisfactorily with today's basic non-postponable mental health problems, and as such it can no longer stand alone as the guiding frame for long-range planning. Reducing the flow of dysfunction is appealing as a conceptual alternative. If we cannot do this, we risk treading water until we drown!

Sharing in common the call for a whole reconceptualization of causation in mental health, a number of models have been proposed—e.g., the Boston Conference community paradigm (Bennett, Anderson, Cooper, Hassol, Klein, and Rosenblum, 1966), Kelly's ecological model (1966), and Albee's continuity-environmental-learning position (1969). Here we are attempting to build on some of the basic tenets and common threads articulated to date by integrating them into what we will refer to as a psychosocial competence–community (PSCC) model. This model offers the mental health system an alternative to the existing medical illness-clinical (MIC) model. Both models include a set of assumptions, values, goals, techniques and complete problem field, theoretical base, setting, and manpower.

The core assumption offered by the PSCC model is that the individual is inextricably and interactively (both reactively and proactively) related to the social system. Human behavior is assumed to be the product of a complex interaction between individual (personalistic, dispositional) variables and systems (structuralistic, situational) variables. Understanding a person requires the study of general psychological processes that link social systems with individual behavior in complex interactions at individual, group, and systems-community levels.

In a PSCC model, the mental health illness dichotomy is no longer viable. Instead, an assumption of continuity is made. Human behavior is defined as a psychosocial learning process. An individual person's behavior is placed on a continuum of response effectiveness based on competence in dealing with personal, situational, developmental, and systems demands. Dysfunctional behavior is conceptualized as the ineffective handling of these demands, resulting either from learning response patterns that were then or are now inadequate to the tasks, or from the lack of an environment in which one could learn competent alternatives. Dysfunctional behavior is not viewed as the private, self-contained "illness" of a sick individual.

These assumptions are based on a consistent set of values, theories, and problem fields. The *values* emphasized in a PSCC model include positive mental health, human growth, the dignity and personhood of every individual, self-determination, and community responsibility. The model derives its *theoretical base* from such areas as the psychology of learning, community psychology, organizational psychology, social psychology, human ecology, general systems theory, human development, and community organization, as well as clinical psychology and personality theory. The model thus reflects an emphasis on the multidisciplinary approaches to understanding and intervening in human behavior. The *problem field* delineated consists of individual-systems interactions, with a multiple focus on the three components and their interactions: the individual, the group or family, and the community or system. Such a model no longer isolates its change focus on the individual, but postulates change as possible at all levels and as affecting all three components and their interactions.

The PSCC model espouses multiple *goals:* improvement of the quality of life of the person, improvement of the quality of the relationship between the individual and the system, and improvement of the social well-being of the community at large. Objectives related to the individual include (1) increasing the individual's ability to create and respond to his life space, to master developmental tasks, and to grow and develop his potentials; and (2) establishing structures and processes that will assist the individual's attempts to live competently in his environment. Objectives in relation to the community or system include (1) focusing on the improvement of those conditions in the system that affect large numbers of people; (2) minimizing and preventing the development of negative factors within the community, i.e., alienation, poverty, racism, discrimination by age or sex; and (3) creating, promoting, and multiplying in the community the kinds of settings, opportunities, and processes that are supportive and that enhance growth and learning consistent with the model's values.

To achieve these goals, the PSCC model proposes a new set of mental health *techniques* to supplement traditional diagnostic and therapeutic skills. This new repertoire includes teaching individuals how to be more effective, competent problemsolvers; training existing community change agents (i.e., indigenous leaders, teachers, police, clergy, bartenders); and providing expertise (i.e., knowledge, skills, research) to community decisionmaking, consultation to community groups and agencies, coordination of community problemsolving and service efforts, community organization, and evaluative research. The sanctioned *setting* for the mental health enterprise is no longer restricted to the hospital or clinic, but extends to community settings that include schools, housing developments, community meetings, police stations, welfare agencies, churches, and so on. The clinic itself is transformed into a mental *health* center that focuses on promotion and prevention as well as care and relearning for the dysfunctional person.

The nature of the roles and the relationship stipulated in the effective implementation of the PSCC model requires a reconceptualization of the professional-client relationship. In the PSCC model, the mental health worker forsakes the mystique of the "healer." Instead, the worker functions in the role of teacher or consultant, affecting change in a jointly shared, cooperative process, advising, suggesting, recommending, teaching problemsolving, modeling, guiding, and learning. The professional's influence is exerted as much through personal credibility, personal resources, partial expertise, energy, and willingness to participate actively as through role status or credentials. In individual, group, and community interventions, the mental health worker calls on the "clients" to be self-determining, responsible, and active in their own learning and change processes. The working alliance is defined as one of partnership, each teaching and learning, each generating and contributing resources, maximizing these in the synergic pooling of problemsolving to produce change.

Such a relationship requires the cultivation of new roles for the mental health professional. Not only is the worker actively involved in the change process, but he is also involved in training other community change agents as "multipliers" of effective change and service delivery. The role model most often articulated within the PSCC model is that of the "participant-conceptualizer."* The mental health worker actively participates in the change process (at individual, group, and community levels), and actively contributes resource and knowledge to decisionmaking, organizing, and change efforts. At the same time, the mental health agent is called upon to step back, to observe, to conceptualize, to generate models, to evaluate, to research, and to feed back this information into the problemsolving process.

TRAINING

The permanence and embellishment of the advances in geropsychology and community psychology are contingent upon more

---

*Kelly (1970) noted: "The phrase 'participant conceptualizer' has become an apt identification for the unique role of the community psychologist. For future archival value, this phrase was first coined by Forrest Tyler ... in group discussions at the Boston University Conference on Community Psychology, Swampscott, Massachusetts, May 5, 1965."

than just professional considerations and debates. Perpetuation of these new advances must be institutionalized in the development of graduate training programs that embody and integrate these areas. In this section, eight principal constructs for a community geropsychology training program are discussed.

1. **Scientist-professional.** A critical foundation for a community geropsychology training model is the scientist-professional model of psychology. This involves training in the integrated expertise of both academic-scientific psychology and professional-applied psychology. Historically this has meant training through the medium of a university-based training program that incorporated conceptual and theoretical developments for the three roles of psychodiagnostician, psychotherapist, and researcher.

2. **Social responsibility.** Tyler and Speisman (1967) called for the embodiment of a social responsibility notion in the scientist-professional model. This new element would require the psychologist to involve himself in an active process of seeking to identify and respond to genuine social needs and, further, to relate effectively his scientific knowledge and professional expertise to societal concerns and problemsolving efforts.

3. **Positive mental health and enhancing the quality of life.** Tyler and Speisman (1967) further note: "This new role rests on conceptions of individual functioning that involve more than a clinical study of an individual. They relate his functioning to his personal history, his surroundings, his society, and his present situation. They emphasize not only concepts of deficit, but also concepts of competence and effectiveness." This construct involves the psychologist in studying the diversity of patterns of effective human functioning and in working with individual and community factors that produce and foster competent problemsolving and positive mental health.

4. **Participant-conceptualizer.** Training in community geropsychology continues as an investment in the scientist-professional model in the form of the participant-conceptualizer. Training experiences provide the faculty and students with clear and active involvement in the change process, but simultaneously demand observation, conceptualization, and theorization within the framework of a PSCC model or other models. This construct is also consistent with the commitment to training experiences that provide

a real service to communities, agencies, and clients involved, that include an evaluation component, and that offer training opportunities for faculty and students.

5. Multiple skills at multiple levels. The training model encourages the learning of intervention skills at multiple levels—individual, group, and systems—across diverse populations. This notion is consistent with the suggestion of the Boston Conference (Bennett et al., 1966) that traning not be limited to any one single method but be geared toward producing a person who is concerned with and capable of assisting with individual issues of competence, self-determination, and personal growth; with group or family dynamics; and with studying and effecting change in social systems. Individuals may choose to focus on developing skills at a particular level—e.g., group techniques—with varied populations or on cultivating general change skills and problemsolving techniques at multiple levels. This principle allows for the appreciation and integration of traditional clinical psychology skills in assessment and psychotherapy. At the same time, it calls for the extended application of these skills and the exploration of new means to provide service to previously neglected populations and to systems or community levels.

6. Multidisciplinary. While training is primarily the responsibility of the clinical-community program, training experiences are designed to promote contact and reciprocal learning among many different groups. Spielberger and Iscoe (1970), Kelly (1966), and the Boston Conference (Bennett et al., 1966) have noted the essential training value of drawing upon the resources, roles, and perspectives of many different fields and populations—other areas of psychology, other academic disciplines (sociology, political science, architecture), and certain vested groups (community residents, social workers, medical workers, politicans).

7. Research. An outgrowth of the commitment to the partici-pant-conceptualizer model is emphasis on research as an indispensable part of the training experience. This priority involves confronting the question of taking psychological research methods and learning research as apprentice-collaborators in ongoing projects, or of developing independent projects.

8. Faculty-student relationships. In keeping with the participant-conceptualizer role model, faculty are encouraged to move beyond

the traditional supervisor-preceptor role and to participate in training and service experiences with graduate students. Just as community interventions are regarded as a shared enterprise involving both mental health professionals and community residents, the training program views faculty and students as colleagues. The training program is able to provide more effective service through the sharing of responsibility and combining of faculty and student resources. Further, such joint programs provide the opportunity for mutual observation and evaluation of real life, ongoing intervention efforts. This arrangement also moves beyond the debilitating dichotomy of training placements that is traditional in the universities.

Iscoe (1971) has made the general comment on community training that "there is a need to acknowledge the uncharted waters that have to be navigated." It is our feeling that the constructs outlined here can begin to provide some reference points for mapping out an effective course.

COMMUNITY GEROPSYCHOLOGY TRAINING AND SERVICE

Mensh, who wrote the community paper in the 1973 APA Task Force on Aging book, agreed that the establishment of community programs is a positive development in terms of aiding the elderly. However, he concluded that community programs generally have been characterized by expeditious, sporadic, haphazard, uncoordinated evolvement, rather than by careful planning based on research, needs assessment, or models of service delivery. We would suggest that the three components just discussed—geropsychology, community psychology, and training—and the common threads running throughout—life span development tasks, competence, individual–social system matrix, participant-conceptualizer role—can begin to provide a systematic alternative model. This alternative community geropsychology model contrasts with the traditional medical-illness–clinical model in psychology and with decrement models in gerontology. It also goes beyond simple community mental health models of service delivery in offering a perspective that can be applied to inpatient and residential programs as well as to community-based or consultative programs.

We would further suggest that a community model seems particularly suitable for psychological intervention with the aged, since they as a group are so much affected by social factors, negative stereotypes, and community processes that discourage their competencies. Although within gerontology there has been some work on the psychosocial and ecological aspects of aging, community psychologists, who usually call for a focus of effort on traditionally neglected segments of the population, have not been addresssing themselves to those special problems and changes necessary for the elderly.

As an example of some ways in which this community model might be applied, we turn to a description of the community-based program of training and service that is currently being implemented in the University of Maryland Clinical-Community Psychology Training Program. One focus involves a coordinated set of interventions in the model neighborhoods area of Prince Georges County. The bridging of community and university needs and resources originates at meetings of the Model Neighborhoods Community Interest Group. This group is made up of representatives from the community, the university, and service agencies who come together in an attempt at reciprocal resource sharing and joint problemsolving.

At one of the monthly interest group meetings last fall, two senior citizens identified the elderly as being part of the population who needed more services than they were getting. In response, the interest group designated a university-community Aging Task Force to look into the problem. The actions now under way as a result of this task force are consistent with the model presented, with interventions directed at individual, group, and system levels.

Historically, our intervention began at the group level around the issue of increasing the effectiveness of the senior citizens club. Our actions have included consultation with regard to group organizational functioning. We are also proposing to add a dimension to the club meetings, using psychodrama and group techniques to assist members in focusing on their concerns, on their handling of life span development tasks, and on their interactions with one another. This group-oriented effort has been supplemented by individual contacts. One avenue has involved working with the two indigenous senior citizen leaders. It was felt that increasing the competence of these individuals would lead to multiplicative beneficial effects on those individuals with whom they worked. Another avenue at the individual level consisted of the informal contacts established through our regularly participating in the senior citizens meetings. A research component on this level is emerging from individual members' willingness to participate in research directed at studying individual personality processes through the life cycle and styles of coping with developmental tasks.

It became clear that we needed to include a systems level effort in the intervention. One effort will be to establish the senior citizens clubs as effective advocacy groups for the model neighborhoods senior citizens residents within the county government system. An aspect of this effort is helping the members of the senior citizens club to get involved in locating other elderly community residents, assessing their needs, and trying to meet these needs through the senior citizens club or other county services.

One of our most creative ventures to date was designed to increase community awareness of senior citizen concerns. Two faculty members and five graduate students attended the annual senior citizen open house, where we stepped out of our usual professional roles to put on a skit that pointed to some of the major concerns of older people and encouraged elderly community residents actively to meet some of their own needs through the senior citizens clubs. Much to our amazement, not only did the skit serve an effective educational function with the senior citizens, with community residents, and with agency workers who were present, but it so impressed the director of the county department of programs and services for the aged that he is trying to send our company "on the road" throughout Prince Georges County. In addition, we are setting up a consultative relationship with the county aging director that may include helping him to implement a program evaluation in his agency.

Another multilevel intervention that grew out of our contacts with the social service agencies in the county occurred when we were invited by the Prince Georges Public Housing Authority to assess both the needs and the effectiveness of the delivery of services to the residents of a rent-subsidized public housing project at Owens Road. In addition to needs assessment, we worked with housing project residents to develop and implement plans to fill gaps in the service delivery system.

In response to expressed need, on the individual level, one of the services we have offered is the opportunity for individual counseling for those who seek help or who are referred to us by the management staff or other community leaders. On the group level, we organized weekly meetings open to all residents. These meetings were devoted to continuing feedback on the problems encountered by the aged in their dealings with the systems of the larger communities, as well as to giving the residents a chance to share the difficulties, frustrations, and joys of living together in this apartment housing community. This group meeting is potentially a vehicle for coordinating various interest groups, such as those planning recreation and social activities, those working on solutions to interpersonal and transportation problems, and those involved in resident governance and health concerns; and for creating a more effective community. On the systems level, we plan to provide feedback to public and private agencies in the county, including the hospitals, and police and welfare departments. This project also serves as a model for a housing project intervention such as might be implemented elsewhere in the county.

In the future, we expect that student-faculty teams will become involved in such other activities as state hospital programs for the aging, halfway houses, and daycare programs. In this regard, the geriatric milieu programs developed at Ypsilanti State Hospital (Coons, 1971) and the Dorothea Dix Hospital Geri-Center (Siegler and Gatz, 1974) are consistent with our general model. These treatment programs are based on creating an environment that fosters self-respect and that, through a series of structured demands, encourages each resident to engage in self-care activities, normal social roles, and independent living to the extent to which he or she is able. This program concept relates to life span developmental and psychosocial competence–community perspectives.

The projects and programs we have described here illustrate the principles and interrelationships presented in the preceding three sections of this chapter and suggest how a community geropsychology model with training and service functions might be implemented. It is important here to underline the PSCC principle of shared responsibility, joint problemsolving, and consultation and collaboration directed toward strengthening the community's own resources. In order to avoid further dehumanizing the old people in our society, programming must be directed not simply toward our providing services for the aged, but rather toward our working together with older people to try to make some changes in stereotypic attitudes and current policies and to implement some programs which meet identified concerns.

In this presentation we have discussed the development of a model—a psychosocial competence–community model—and its application to the aging population. The same general PSCC training and service model may be applied to diverse populations—preschoolers, delinquents, and other groups. Although each population has some important unique strengths and unique problems, the same overall model and general principles of change may be applied. In other words, we would like to suggest that we are not just developing a specific model for old people but that we are in some ways proposing a human model for all people.

We might sum it all up with an analogy of the community as a spaceship.* Just as we are all part of the community, we are all on the spaceship together. We are all on the same voyage with a common destination. If we want to get the spaceship off the ground and get it going somewhere, we have to get all the burners going. Different groups of people on the spaceship might be thought of as burners, as potential energy. What often happens on the spaceship is that some of the burners get turned off and defined as ballast, and the rest of the people on the spaceship want to jettison them. This is what has been happening with the aged. Instead, we should be defining everyone, including older persons, as having energy to contribute. Thus, we can utilize the energy from all the sources, and insure that we reach our destination together.

REFERENCES

Albee, G. Relation of conceptual models of disturbed behavior to institutional and manpower requirements. In F. Arnoff, E. Rubenstein, and J. Speisman, *Manpower for mental health*. Chicago: Aldine Publishing Co., 1969.

Bennett, C.C.; Anderson, I.S.; Cooper, S.; Hassol, L.; Klein, D.; and Rosenblum, G. *Community psychology* (Boston Conference). Boston: Boston University Press, 1966.

Chiribogo, D. Perceptions of well being. Paper presented at American Psychological Association Convention, New Orleans, 1974.

Coons, D. Special problems of mentally ill aged and their response to a therapeutic community. Paper presented at American Psychological Association Convention, Washington, D.C., 1971.

Cowen, E. Social and community interventions. In P. Mussen, and S. Rosenzweig, *Annual review of psychology*, vol. 24, Palo Alto, California: Annual Reviews Inc., 1973.

Dohrenwend, B.P. and Dohrenwend, B.S. *Social status and psychological disorder: A casual inquity*. New York: Wiley-Interscience, 1969.

Eisdorfer, C. Mental health in later life. In S.E. Golann, and C. Eisdorfer, *Handbook of community mental health*. New York: Appleton-Century-Crofts, 1972.

Eisdorfer, C. and Lawton, M.P. eds., *The psychology of adult development and aging*. Washington, D.C.: American Psychological Association, 1973.

Gottesman, L.E.; Quarterman, C.E.; and Cohn, G.M. Psychosocial treatment of the aged. In C. Eisdorfer, and M.P. Lawton, *The psychology of adult development and aging*. Washington, D.C.: American Psychological Association, 1973.

Havighurst, R.J. *Developmental tasks and education*. 3rd ed., New York: David McKay Company, Inc., 1972.

*The spaceship metaphor was created by Ken Patton and Don Hurley of the University of Maryland.

Iscoe, I. Professional and subprofessional training in community mental health as an aspect of community psychology. In Task Force on Community Mental Health, Division 27 of APA, *Issues in community psychology and preventive mental health.* New York: Behavioral Publications, 1971.

James, G. Adapting urban mental health services to our aging population *American Journal of Orthopsychiatry,* 1964, *34:* 840-51.

Kelly, J. Ecological constraints on mental health services. *American Psychologist,* 1966, *21:* 535-39.

———. The quest for valid preventive interventions. In C. Spielberger, *Current topics in clinical and community psychology.* Vol. 2., New York.: Academic Press, 1970.

Kent, D.P.; Kastenbaum, R.; and Sherwood, S., eds. *Research planning and action for the elderly.* New York: Behavioral Publications, 1972.

Kramer, M.; Taube, C.A.; and Redick, R.W. Patterns of use of psychiatric facilities by the aged: past, present, and future. In C. Eisdorfer and M.P. Lawton, *The psychology of adult development and aging.* Washington, D.C.: American Psychological Association, 1973.

Lawton, M.P. Clinical psychology. In C. Eisdorfer and M.P. Lawton, *The psychology of adult development and aging.* Washington, D.C.: American Psychological Association, 1973.

Mensh, I.N. Community mental health and other health services for the aged. In C. Eisdorfer and M.P. Lawton, *The psychology of adult development and aging.* Washington, D.C.: American Psychological Association, 1973.

Neugarten, B.L. Personality change in late life: a developmental perspective. In C. Eisdorfer and M.P. Lawton eds., *The psychology of adult development and aging.* Washington, D.C.: American Psychological Association, 1973, 311-35.

———. What does successful aging mean? Successful aging in 1970 and 1990. In Pfeiffer, E., ed. *Successful aging.* A Conference Report. Durham, North Carolina: Duke University Center for the Study of Aging and Human Development, 1974.

Research on Aging Act, 1973. Report No. 93-299 GPO Stock #5270-01926.

Schaie, K.W. A reinterpretation of age related changes in cognitive structure and functioning. In L.R. Goulet and P.B. Baltes, *Life-span developmental psychology: Research and theory.* New York: Academic Press, 1970.

Siegler, I.C. and Gatz, M. Evaluation of the Dix Geri-Center: the first nine months. Grant report. North Carolina Department of Mental Health, Raleigh, North Carolina, 1974.

Smith, M. and Hobbs, N. The community mental health center. *American Psychologist,* 1966, *21:* 499-509.

Spielberger, C.D. and Iscoe, I. The current status of training in community psychology. In I. Iscoe and C.D. Spielberger, *Community psychology: Perspectives in training and research.* New York: Appleton-Century-Crofts, 1970.

Taber, M. and Flynn, M. Social policy and social provision for the elderly in the 1970's. *The Gerontologist,* 1971, *11:* 41-54.

Tyler, F.B. and Speisman, J.C. An emerging scientist-professional role in psychology. *American Psychologist,* 1967, *22:* 839-47.

※ *Chapter 8*

Clinical Gerontology: A Proposed Curriculum

June E. Blum
Post Graduate Center for Mental Health

> If God grant me old age
> I would see some things finished; some
> outworn;
> Some stone prepared for builders yet
> unborn,
> Nor would I be the sated, weary sage
> Who sees no strange new wonder in
> each morn.
>
> Burges Johnson

In the lines above, Johnson personally expressed the dynamic process of *growing* old, rather than the static concept of being old. The static concept subscribed to by many was supported by data that depicted older persons as rigid, inept, cantankerous, and as having outlived their usefulness (Hamlin, 1967; Lewis and Butler, 1972). In sum, it supported the myths and stereotypes that have gradually given the elders the status of an oppressed minority group in our culture, and it has contributed to their being provided with minimal psychological services.

The principal source of these data emanated from the captive population of the institutions, in particular, the Veterans Administration's aging patients (Coppinger, 1967). Recent statistics reveal, however, that only 5 percent of our older people (65 years or older) are actually in institutions or nursing homes (Berezin, 1972; Buss and

Pfeiffer, 1970). Of the remaining 95 percent of community residents, 81 percent have no limitations on their mobility. What of them?

The oldest longitudinal study on senescence (Kallmann and Jarvik, 1959; Jarvik, 1967; Blum, Clark and Jarvik, in press; Blum and Jarvik, 1974) addressed itself to community living subjects. The project was initiated by Lissy Jarvik and the late Franz Kallmann in 1947 to study the hereditary effects of aging and longevity (Kallman and Sander, 1949). The subjects were twins, who were at least 60 years of age at their initial testing. The results relating to intellectual stability, and those emanating from studies at the Duke University Center for Aging and Human Development, revealed a classical pattern of aging, of a progressive decline in performance on speeded tasks and, given good health, maintenance of intellectual abilities well into the eighth decade (Jarvik, Eisdorfer, and Blum, 1973). The data appear to challenge the notion of a generalized "declining intelligence" of the elderly depicted in the earlier studies on institutionalized patients. Hence, the impetus for applied clinical gerontology resides within these research results. Nevertheless, a review of gerontology shows that the majority of services are geared to studying or doing something for the "aged" as a population, not as individuals. Until recently, the subjective, intrapsychic aspects of aging persons have been essentially overlooked.

The term *individual* is stressed here, for individual differences are spoken of and researched in reference to children and adolescents. As one climbs the chronological ladder, however, the theory of individual differences tends to be replaced by the notion of a conglomerate called the *aged*. This is a specious notion indeed, for aged people deemed "individual" at birth have, in addition, been subjected to diversified life experiences, values, and stresses, compounded by variations in education, religion, income, geographic residence, and subculture. There may well be greater variability among the elderly than in any other cohort group. It thus becomes our mandate to vitiate the misconceptions and strengthen our services to older adults by extending the scope of clinical programs to include the psychodynamics of the later years. Such training would involve problems of dynamic aging, and as a matter of course, would be concerned with life cycle behavioral adaptations.

PROPOSED CURRICULUM

The focus of the training program envisioned would encompass *prevention*, *intervention*, and *rehabilitation*, with community-living older adults as well as the fragile elderly residing in nursing homes and institutions who are beset by lifelong unresolved intrapsychic conflict and/or by reactions due to traumata specific to aging, e.g. loss of narcissistic supplies, retirement, reduced capacities, and role changes. The proposed training curriculum would comprise theoretical courses and clinical and research experience. The suggested areas are: (1) psychodynamics of the life cycle, (2) differential diagnosis and therapeutic intervention, and (3) delivery and evaluation of community services to older adults. In each case, specific content material for courses suggested below would be derived from work outlined in earlier chapters in this volume, as well as from literature noted in the Appendix, pertaining to the psychodynamic considerations of the life cycle. The integration of the aforementioned would equip the prospective clinical gerontologist to meet the challenges suggested by Gottesman in Chapter One. Specifically, the course content would be the following:

Psychodynamics of the Life Cycle

This section is deemed primary because it indicates that aging does not exist in a vacuum. It is part of the developmental scheme of life, a fact which has largely been ignored. Division 20 of the American Psychological Association emphasized this developmental continuum only as recently as 1970, when its name was changed from "Maturity and Old Age" to "Adult Development and Aging."

1. A survey course would present an *overview of gerontology* with projections for the future; certainly the aging of yesterday are not the aging of today or of tomorrow. An adjunct to this course would pertain the the *biological-sociological* and *psychological* aspects of aging. The basic tenet of this section is presented in Dr. Siegler's chapter (see Chapter Six), and the contributions of Birren et al. (1959) and Eisdorfer and Lawton (1973), as well as Maddox (1971), Jeffers (1969), Lewis (1975), Lowenfeld (1975), and those of Kreps (1962) and Shanas and Streib (1965).

2. In cognizance of the necessity that *personality theories* be viewed from a life span approach, the work of Freud, Jung, Adler, Hartmann, Erikson, Klein, and Guntrip, and other major theorists would be explored, as well as the contributions of gerontologists including Kuhlen, Buhler, Linden, Neugarten, Berezin, Cath, Kastenbaum, and so forth. Interestingly, Freud suggested that "near or about the fifties the elasticity of the mental processes, on which treatment depends, is as a rule lacking—old people are no longer educable" (Freud, 1924). The dissidents include Abraham, Kaufman, and Atkinson (Rechtschaffen, 1959). Jung went further by differentiating the tasks of those in the early years and those in later

years. For the Jungian, the task of senescence concerns individualization—Dr. Shows (see Chapter Five) addresses himself specifically to Jung's theory and his therapeutic approach with older people. Inherent in the aforementioned theories are the conceptualizations of what would be considered *"normal development."* As Freud garnered his data from abnormal behavior and extrapolated to the normal, so gerontologists, too, as noted, initially focused on institutionalized populations. A reformulation of "normal development" determined from the study of noninstitutionalized populations would be emphasized as vital to our understanding of personality throughout the life span. Writings including Palmore (1970, 1974), and Zinberg and Kaufman (1963) would be discussed.

3. Deviations from the norm or abnormal aging behavior would be explored in a course on *psychopathology of the aging process.* The specific categories include: I. *neuroses*—anxiety neurosis, obsessive-compulsive and phobic neuroses, depressive neuroses, hysteria, neurasthenia, and hypochrondriacal reactions; II. *organic syndromes* — (a) reversible brain disorder; (b) chronic brain syndrome; (i) senile psychosis; (ii) presenile dementia (Alzheimer's disease and Pick's disease); and III. *functional psychoses*—(a) mood disorders:—affective psychoses (psychotic depression reaction and manic depressive psychoses); (b) thought disorders:—schizophrenia, paranoid psychoses of late life (late life paraphrenia). The classifications as enumerated are viewed as separate entities for nosological purposes. In the later years, as throughout the life span, one disorder may mask another and/or be symptomatic of it.

In addition, the implication of themes such as alienation, loneliness, loss of role, grief, and fear of dying as components and/or precipitators of maladaptive behavior would be considered. References would include the contributions of Butler and Lewis (1973), Levin and Kahana (1967), Busse and Pfeiffer (1973), and Verwoerdt (1976).

Differential Diagnosis and
Therapeutic Interventions

Psychodiagnostic training and treatment planning sensitive to the older patient's diagnosis is crucial to the training of the clinical gerontologist.

1. Here, issues of differential diagnosis are paramount. For example, discrimination between primary depression and depression that is secondary to a physical disorder is an essential diagnostic consideration in the elderly, as is differential diagnosis between a depression that mimics features of organic brain dysfunction

(confusion and retarded thinking), and primary cerebral deterioration. In addition to organic and psychogenic considerations, a diagnosis must be sensitive to the implications of a patient's demographic uniqueness. The chapter in this volume by Bernal et al. (see Chapter Four) addresses these issues, along with those of selection of test instruments, test administration, norms for the older persons, and overall usefulness of psychodiagnosis for the elderly. The role of psychological tests is also discussed by Butler and Lewis (1973) and Ames et al. (1973) as part of the general diagnostic evaluation of older persons. Interdisciplinary collaboration between the fields of psychology, psychiatry, medicine, and social work comes to the fore in issues relating to diagnosis and treatment of the elderly and in training programs providing such an experience.

2. Basic to the curriculum would be courses concerned with *techniques of psychotherapy*, *clinical practice* with patients who represent a cross-section of the life cycle, and *supervision* of the trainee's caseload. Each trainee should have the opportunity of working with patients for whom medication is a co-treatment modality, and to learn the essentials of *psychopharmacology of the older adult*. *Treatment modalities* would include individual therapy, group therapy, counseling, crisis intervention and utilization of community resources. Rehabilitation techniques such as behavioral modification will be presented as a means of activating a fragile patient, and possibly vitiating progressive deterioration. Here, references to the writings of Grotjahn (1951), Krasner (1974), Oberleder (1970), Goldfarb (1968), and Linden (1957) would be made.

Family treatment, which has earned recognition as a viable treatment modality, has positive value for the three generational family (Spark and Brody, 1970). The course would concern concepts of family development and organization. The inclusion of grandparents is crucial to the understanding of family psychodynamics, and preventive measures would be implemented by intervention in a legacy of pathological interation. Techniques for working through distortions, myths, and guilt would be investigated.

Delivery and Evaluation of Community
Services to the Elder Adult

1. A *practicum in community mental health* would be included to aid the trainee in translating his skills to meet the ever-increasing mental health needs of the aging population who reside in the community. The basic theory, principles, and techniques of community mental health consultation would be presented. Again, learning by doing would be stressed. Individual projects relating to

the improvement of the quality of life and delivery of services to the aging by specific groups, centers, agencies, institutions, and nursing homes would be selected.

2. *Research in community mental health* would represent a course concerned with methods and techniques for investigating mental health problems and needs of elderly residing in the community, as well as a means for evaluating therapeutic efforts for this population.

3. Finally, a *laboratory in group experience* would be a basic curriculum item that, in essence, is the bedrock of a clinical practice as well as of community living. This experience would allow the future clinical gerontologist to explore his own motives and attitudes toward aging and to work through misconceptions and prejudices in a process of critical self-evaluation.

This course could utilize the empathic model (University of Michigan), which would experientially provide the trainees with the sensory loss continuum experienced by the aging and the elderly. For example, the trainees would be provided with lens thickened for the average 75 year old eye, ear plugs to simulate hearing loss encountered through the aging process, and plastic fingers simulating reduced tactile sense. They would, thus, be sensitized on a first-hand basis to some of the physiological changes associated with aging, and would be able to examine their reactions to same in a group setting. Aged volunteers from the community might act as co-participants in the groups, with the aim of sharing their own experiences and co-operatively maximizing the rapport between generations.

The curriculum, as sketched, is ideally adaptable for a multidisciplinary (M.D., Ph.D., M.S.W.) mental health training center such as the Postgraduate Center for Mental Health, which has departments of specialization ranging from child to adolescent to adult. Although trainees specialize in one of the particular departments, their program is not an isolated one. The laboratory experience would be an integral part of their curriculum, for the specialized departments are representative of specific aspects of life, while the aging process is life.

As the postgraduate center is dedicated to training, practice, research, and community mental health consulation, training is adapted to meet the needs of those at various phases of career development—i.e., the psychoanalyst-psychotherapist, adjunct professionals (physicians, dentists, lawyers, educators, etc.), the mental health counselor, and school aides. Thus, this laboratory experience and the curriculum itself can be accommodated to meet the needs of those at various levels of training for service in community mental health and in our educational system. In particular, the experiential laboratory could be included in the curriculum modules now being prepared for the secondary schools by the National Science Foundation. The resultant inter- and intrapsychic experiences could pave the way for the demise of agism more than as a didactic lesson plan.

An ivory tower curriculum is not contemplated. There must be an ongoing integration of theory and practice. However, this is one airplane that will not leave the ground until attitudes toward the aging are redefined. Gerontologists must develop a practical socio-therapy addressed to productively altering the attitudes toward the aging by the clinicians, patients, and society at large—a large order.

To attain this end, an interdisciplinary rapprochement is mandated. Aging is for all. Indeed, as Pogo might say it: "The Aging is Us!"

REFERENCES

Ames, L.B., Metraux, R.W.; Rodell, J.L.; and Walker, R.N. *Rorschach responses in old age*. New York: Brummer/Mazel, 1973.

Berezin, M.A. Psychodynamic considerations of aging and the aged: An overview. *American Journal of Psychiatry*, 1972, *12:* 33–41.

Birren, J. et al., eds. *Handbook of aging and the individual*. Chicago: University of Chicago Press, 1959.

Blum, J.E. and Jarvik, L.F. Intellectual performance of octogenarians as a function of education and initial ability. *Human Development*, 1974, *17:* 364–75.

Blum, J.E.; Clark, E.T.; and Jarvik, L.F. *Intellectual functioning of adults: psychological and biological influences*. New York: Springer, in press.

Busse, E.W. and Pfeiffer, E. Functional psychiatric disorders in old age. In E.W. Busse & E. Pfeiffer, eds., *Behavior and adaptation in late life*, pp. 183–235. Boston: Little Brown, 1970.

Busse, E.W. and Pfeiffer, E. *Mental illness in later life*. Washington, D.C.: American Psychiatric Association, 1973.

Butler, R.N. and Lewis, M.I. *Aging and mental health*. St. Louis, Mo.: Mosby, 1973.

Coppinger, N.W. Introduction. *The Gerontologist*, 1967, 7: 1–2.

Eisdorfer, C. and Lawton, P., eds. *The psychology of adult development and Aging*. Washington, D.C.: American Psychological Association, 1973.

Freud, S. On psychotherapy. *Collected Papers*. Vol. I. London: Hogarth Press, 1924.

Goldfarb, A.I. Clinical perspectives. *Psychiatric Research Papers*, American Psychiatric Association, February 1968.

Grotjahn, M. Some psychoanalytic observations about the process of growing old. In G. Roheim, ed., *Psychoanalysis and social sciences*, vol 3, pp. 301–312. New York: International Universities Press, 1951.

Hamlin, R.M. A utility theory of old age. *The Gerontologist*, 1967, 7: 35-45.

Jarvik, L.F. Survival and psychological aspects of aging in man. *Symposium on Social and Experimental Biology*, 1967, *21*: 463-82.

Jarvik, L.F.: Eisdorfer, C.; and Blum, J.E. *Intellectural functioning in adults.* New York: Springer, 1973.

Jeffers, F.C., ed. *Proceedings of Seminars of the Duke University Council on Aging and Human Development: 1965-69.* Durham, N.C.: Duke University Medical Center, 1969.

Kallman, F.J. and Jarvik, L.F. Individual differences in constitution and genetic background. In J.E. Birren, ed., *Handbook of aging and the individual,* pp. 216-63. Chicago: University of Chicago Press, 1959.

Kallman, F.J. and Sander, G. Twin studies on senescence. *American Journal of Psychiatry*, 1949, *106*: 29-36.

Krasner, J.D. Analytic group psychotherapy with the aged. In Stefan de Schill, ed., *The challenge for group psychotherapy: Present and future.* New York: International Universities Press, 1974.

Kreps, J.M. *Employment, income and retirement problems of the aged.* Durham, N.C.: Duke University Press, 1962.

Levin, S. and Kahana, R.J. *Psychodynamic studies on aging: Creativity, reminiscing, and dying.* New York: International Universities Press, 1967.

Lewis, J.A. *Law and aging: A conference report.* Durham, N.C.: Duke University Center for the Study of Aging and Human Development, 1975.

Lewis, M.I. and Butler, R.N. Why is women's lib ignoring old women? *Aging and Human Development*, 1972, 2: 223-31.

Linden, M.E. The promise of therapy in the emotional problems of aging. 4th Congress, International Association of Gerontology, Italy, 1957.

Lowenthal, M.F., et al. *Four stages of life.* San Francisco: Jossey-Bass, 1975.

Maddox, G.L. ed., *The future of aging and the aged.* Atlanta: SMPA Foundation Seminar Books, 1971.

Oberleder, M. Crisis therapy in mental breakdown of the aging. *The Gerontologist*, 1970, *10*(2): 111-14.

Palmore, E., ed., *Normal aging I.* Durham, N.C.: Duke University Press, 1970.

———. *Normal Aging II.* Durham, N.C.: Duke University Press, 1974.

Rechtschaffen, A. Psychotherapy with geriatric patients: A review of the literature. *Journal of Gerontology*, 1959, *14B*(1): 73-83.

Shanas, E. and Streib, G., eds. *Social structure and the family.* Englewood Cliffs, N.J.: Prentice-Hall, 1965.

Spark, G. and Brody, E.M. The aged are family members. *Family Process*, 1970, *9*(2): 195-210.

Verwoerdt, A. *Clinical geropsychiatry.* Baltimore: Williams & Wilkins, 1976.

Zinberg, N.E. and Kaufman, I., eds., *Normal psychology of the aging process.* New York: International Universities Press, 1963.

Appendix

JOURNALS

Black Aging
National Council on Black Aging, Inc.
Box 8522
Durham, North Carolina 27707

British Journal of Geriatric Practice
Stuart Phillips Publications
Suffolk House
Copse Hill, Sutton,
Surrey, England

Educational Gerontology
Hemisphere Publishing Corporation
1025 Vermont Ave., N.W.
Washington, D.C. 20005

Experimental Aging Research
Box 85
Bar Harbor, Maine 04609

Experimental Gerontology
Pergamon Press, Inc.
Maxwell House, Fairview Park
Elmsford, New York 10523

Geriatrics
4015 W. 65th Street
Minneapolis, Minnesota 55435

Geriatrics Digest
Geriatrics Digest Inc.
444 Frontage Road
Northfield, Illinois 60093

Gerontologist
Gerontological Society
1 Dupont Circle
Number 520
Washington, D.C. 20036

International Journal of Aging & Human Development
Baywood Publishing Co.
43 Central Drive
Farmingdale, New York 11735

Journal of Geriatric Psychiatry
International Universities Press
New York, New York

Journal of the American Geriatrics Society
American Geriatrics Society
10 Columbus Circle
New York, New York 10019

Journal of Gerontology
Gerontological Society
1 Dupont Circle
Number 520
Washington, D.C. 20036

BOOKS — General

Baltes, P.B. & Schaie, K.W. *Life-span developmental psychology: personality and socialization.* New York: Academic Press, 1973.

Birren, J.E. *Handbook of aging and the individual.* Chicago: University of Chicago Press, 1959.

Birren, J.E., Butler, R.N., Greenhouse, S.W., Sokoloff, L. & Yarrow, M.R. *Human Aging I: a biological and behavioral study.* DHEW Publication Number (ADM) 74-122, 1974.

Botwinick, J. *Aging and behavior.* New York: Springer, 1973.

Butler, R.N. & Lewis, M.I. *Aging & mental health: positive psychological approaches.* St. Louis: C.V. Mosby, 1973.

Cummings, E. & Henry, W.E. *Growing old: the process of disengagement.* New York: Basic Books, 1961.

Datan, N. & Ginsberg, L.H. *Life-span developmental psychology: normative life crises.* New York: Academic Press, 1975.

Eisdorfer, C. & Lawton, M.P. *The psychology of adult development and aging.* Washington, D.C.: American Psychological Association, 1973.

Goulet, L.R. & Baltes, P.B. *Life-span developmental psychology: research and theory.* New York: Academic Press, 1970.

Granick, S. & Patterson, R.D. *Human aging II: an eleven-year followup biological and behavioral study.* DHEW Publication Number (ADM) 74-123, 1974.

Jarvik, L.F., Eisdorfer, C., & Blum, J.E. *Intellectual functioning in adults.* New York: Springer, 1973.

Kastenbaum, R. *New thoughts on old age.* New York: Springer, 1971.

Kent, D.P., Kastenbaum, R., & Sherwood, S. *Research planning and action for the elderly.* New York: Behavioral Publications, 1972.

Lowenthal, M.F., Thurnher, M., & Chiriboga, D. *Four stages of life.* San Francisco: Jossey-Bass, 1975.

Maas, H.S. & Kuypers, J.A. *From thirty to seventy.* San Francisco: Jossey-Bass, 1974.

Nesselroade, J.R. & Reese, H.W. *Life-span developmental psychology: methodological issues.* New York: Academic Press, 1973.

Neugarten, B.L. *Middle age and aging: a reader in social psychology.* Chicago: University of Chicago Press, 1968.

Neugarten, B.L. & associates. *Personality in middle and late life.* New York: Atherton, 1964.

Schaie, K.W. *Theory and methods of research on aging.* Morgantown, West Virginia: University of West Virginia Press, 1968.

Talland, G.A. *Human aging and behavior.* New York: Academic Press, 1968.

Zinberg, N.E. & Kaufman, I. *Normal psychology of the aging process.* New York: International Universities Press, 1963.

BOOKS — From the Center for the Study of Aging and Human Development, Duke University.

Busse, E.W. & Pfeiffer, E. *Behavior and adaptation in late life.* Boston: Little, Brown, 1970.

Busse, E.W. & Pfeiffer, E. *Mental illness in late life.* Washington, D.C.: American Psychiatric Association, 1973.

Jeffers, F.C. *Guidelines for an information and counselling service for older persons.* Durham, N.C.: Duke University Center for the Study of Aging and Human Development, 1970.

Maddox, G.L. *The future of aging and the aged.* Durham, N.C.: Duke University Center for the Study of Aging and Human Development, 1971.

Palmore, E. *Normal aging I.* Durham, N.C.: Duke University Press, 1970.

Palmore, E. *Normal aging II.* Durham, N.C.: Duke University Press, 1974.

Palmore, E. *Prediction of life span.* Lexington, Mass.: D.C. Heath, 1974.

Pfeiffer, E. *Successful aging.* Durham, N.C.: Duke University Center for the study of Aging and Human Development, 1973.

About the Contributors

Cynthia Belar, Ph.D. is currently an Assistant Professor of Clinical Psychology and Director of Internship Training at the J. Hillis Miller Medical Center, University of Florida. She received her doctoral degree in 1974 from Ohio University and completed a predoctoral internship at Duke University Medical Center. Her interests include medical psychology, adult psychopathology, and psychodiagnostics.

Guillermo A.A. Bernal is a candidate in the doctoral program in clinical psychology at the University of South Carolina. He is an Instructor in the Division of Medical Psychology, Department of Psychiatry, Duke University Medical Center, and Assistant Director of the Clinical Biofeedback Laboratory at Duke Hospital. His professional interests include psychosomatic medicine, psychotherapy, and psychological assessment.

Linda J. Brannon, Ph.D. is currently an Associate in Medical Psychology at Highland Hospital, a division of the Department of Psychiatry, Duke University Medical Center. She received her doctoral degree from Pennsylvania State University in 1976. Her interests include aging, developmental psychology, and psychological assessment.

June E. Blum, Ph.D. is a gerontologist-psychoanalyst-researcher at the Postgraduate Center for Mental Health, New York. She is co-author of two texts in the field of aging entitled INTELLEC·

TUAL FUNCTIONING IN ADULTS and INTELLECTUAL FUNC-TIONING IN ADULTS: PSYCHOLOGICAL AND BIOLOGICAL INFLUENCES, as well as numerous scientific papers. Her professional activities are aimed at training and clinical service in a multi-disciplinary program for meeting the needs of the elderly, i.e. medical, social, psychological, etc. She is a member of numerous professional organizations including the Gerontological Society and Division 20 of the American Psychological Association "Adult Development and Aging".

Roy Cameron, Ph.D. is an Assistant Professor of Psychology at the University of Saskatchewan, with a joint appointment in the University Psychological Services Clinic. His activities include super-vision of graduate students in psychodiagnostics and therapy and research in areas such as biofeedback, cognitive behavior modifica-tion, and self-regulation.

Joseph R. Cautela, Ph.D. is currently Professor of Psychology at Boston College and is involved in private practice, specializing in behavior therapy. He received his doctoral degree from Boston College in 1954 and has remained on that faculty ever since. He has been a Visiting Professor at the Max Planck Institute of Psychi-atry, has served as a consultant to numerous mental health institu-tions, hospitals, and health care facilities. He has over sixty publications in the field of behavior therapy and is a Past-President of the Association for the Advancement of Behavior Therapy. He is also a member of the Gerontological Society.

Margaret J. Gatz, Ph.D. is currently an Assistant Professor of Psychology at the University of Maryland. She received her doctoral degree from Duke University in 1972 and completed her predoc-toral internship at the Department of Behavioral Medicine and Psychiatry, West Virginia University Medical Center and Robert F. Kennedy Youth Center. While at Duke University between 1972 and 1973, she was a postdoctoral research fellow in the Center for the Study of Aging and Human Development and a Lecturer in Psychology at the Duke University Law School. She has authored numerous papers in the field of aging, community mental health, law, and psychodiagnostic assessment. She was conference co-or-dinator for the University of Maryland Fifth Annual Community Clinical Workshop on "Positive Mental Health: Enhancing Human Effectiveness over the Lifespan," 1975.

W. Doyle Gentry, Ph.D. is currently Professor and Head of the Division of Medical Psychology, Department of Psychiatry, Duke University Medical Center. He is also a Lecturer in the Psychology Department at Duke University and Senior Fellow in the Duke University Center for the Study of Aging and Human Development. He received his doctoral degree from Florida State University in 1969 and has been on the faculty of Duke University Medical Center since that time. In addition to geropsychology, his clinical and research interests include psychosomatic medicine, human and infrahuman aggression, and behavior therapy. He has authored numerous publications in scientific and professional journals and is editor of APPLIED BEHAVIOR MODIFICATION and co-editor of PSYCHOLOGICAL ASPECTS OF MYOCARDIAL INFARCTION AND CORONARY CARE.

Leonard E. Gottesman, Ph.D. is currently Senior Research Psychologist at the Philadelphia Geriatric Center. Prior to this, he was on the teaching faculty of the University of Michigan. He is a member of both the Gerontological Society and Division 20 of the American Psychological Association. He has published many papers and chapters in books dealing with the needs of the elderly with respect to psychological services, the plight of the aged in state institutions, and the status of the aged in nursing homes.

Gurudershan Singh Nagel is a graduate student in the Clinical-Community Psychology Program at the University of Maryland.

Dan Hurley is a graduate student in the Clinical-Community Psychology Program at the University of Maryland.

Robert L. Kahn, Ph.D. is currently an Associate Professor in the Department of Psychiatry and Human Development at the University of Chicago. He received his master's degree from Columbia University in 1946 and his doctoral degree from New York University in 1953. Since then, he has taught on the faculties of Brooklyn College and Hunter College, has been a consultant to the Home for Aged and Infirm Hebrews of New York, has served as Head of the Psychology Section at Montefiore Hospital, and as a faculty member of the University of Southern California Gerontology Society Center Summer Institute. He is a Fellow in the Gerontological Society and a Diplomate in Clinical Psychology. He has authored over eighty papers to professional journals and is co-author of DENIAL OF ILLNESS: SYMBOLIC AND PHYSIOLOGICAL ASPECTS. His interests include community mental health, geropsychology, and the sociopsychological aspects of psychiatric treatment.

John V. Lavigne, Ph.D. is currently a staff psychologist at Children's Memorial Hospital, Chicago, and an Adjunct Assistant Professor at Northwestern Medical School. He received his doctoral degree from the University of Texas in 1974, after completing his predoctoral internship at Duke University Medical Center, and was an Associate in Medical Psychology in the Department of Psychiatry at Duke Medical School during 1974-75. His professional interests include behavior therapy, pediatric consultation, development of assessment techniques for use with pediatric populations, and family therapy.

George L. Maddox, Ph.D. is currently Director of the Center for the Study of Aging and Human Development at Duke University. He is also Professor of Sociology, Duke University, and Professor and Head of the Division of Medical Sociology, Department of Psychiatry, Duke University Medical Center. He is President-elect of the Gerontological Society and a member and officer of the International Association of Gerontology. He has authored and edited five books including THE FUTURE OF AGING AND THE AGED and DRUG ISSUES IN GEROPSYCHIATRY, in addition to over sixty published papers, chapters, book reviews, and technical reports. He has served as a consultant to the Social Security Administration and the White House Conference on Aging and is a member of the National Advisory Council on Aging, National Institutes of Health.

Linda Mansfield is a doctoral candidate at Boston College in the Community and Social Psychology program, with a concentration in behavior modification. Her interests include the application of the behavioral model to problems of the aged.

W. Derek Shows, Ph.D. is currently an Assistant Professor of Medical Psychology in the Department of Psychiatry, Duke University Medical Center. He received a master's degree in classical philology from the University of Illinois, was a Fulbright Fellow at the University of Heidelberg, and received his doctoral degree in clinical psychology from Duke University in 1967. In 1975, he spent a sabattical leave at the C.G. Jung Institut in Zurich, Switzerland. He has been Director of Internship Training in the Division of Medical Psychology at Duke University Medical Center and is currently a Lecturer in the Departments of Psychology and Religion at Duke University. He has numerous scientific and professional publications and his interests include theory and methods of psychotherapy, psychological training, and aging.

Ilene C. Siegler, Ph.D. is currently an Assistant Professor of Medical Psychology in the Department of Psychiatry, Duke University Medical Center and Coordinator of the Research Training Programs in Adult Development and in Aging in the Duke University Center for the Study of Aging and Human Development. She received her doctoral degree from Syracuse University in 1972 and completed a postdoctoral fellowship in aging at Duke University in 1974. She is a member of several professional organizations including the Gerontological Society and has published several scientific papers dealing with aging and developmental psychology.